Empowerment Through Knowledge Presents:

Why Real Men Drink Straight Tequila

The Tao of Chivalry

A Handbook for Men Who Love Men in the New Millennium

RAINBOW EDITION

Eric Thurnbeck &

Sarina Stone

Distributed in the United States by Empowerment Through Knowledge Publishing.

Logo, Cover Art, Layout and Design by Stan O'Daffer.
Illustrations by Eric Thurnbeck
First Printing: October 2014
Library of Congress Catalog Card: Pending
US ISBN 978-0-9826384-9-1
All Rights Reserved.

Table of Contents

Dedications

Sarina's Dedication

This book is dedicated to my brothers who openly love and accept love in return, and Grandmaster Mantak Chia, a man who confidently wears a pink tracksuit while smiling to his heart.

Eric's Dedication

This book is for the men who have known my heart.
To all of the friends and lovers who have shaped my growth over the years, I wouldn't understand chivalry without you.

Acknowledgements

Sarina Stone wishes to thank the following for their contributions:

Stan O'Daffer for tireless publishing and artistic flair.

R. Mordant Mahon for donating the final chapter and asking nothing in return. Thanks, bro.

Eric Thurnbeck for putting his heart and soul in to this book and blowing my mind with perfect graphics.

Grandmaster Mantak Chia for setting me on the Taoist path.

Sarina's Introduction

When I boarded the plane for Phoenix to start this manuscript with Eric, I knew this book was going to be different.

My name is Sarina Stone, and I am a speaker on the subject of natural health and a Medical Chi Kung instructor. I teach people how to use their minds to facilitate positive changes in their bodies. This does not replace your doctor; it helps you to participate in the healing process. In recent years, I have also become an author. I write about romantic intimacy and conscious relationships. Relationships need to be discussed in my industry because they are one of the things that make people so passionate that, for better or worse, it actually affects their heath.

The first Why Real Men Drink Straight Tequila book was written for heterosexual men. I had a ball working with Eric, but over the course of many months I began to realize that a huge group of men were excluded from the material because it only spoke of male/female interaction. I saw that in a same-sex relationship, Yin and Yang – masculine and feminine – qualities also exist. They are so pervasive at times that we don't even realize we have taken on these roles with each other. Yes, I know, sometimes the masculine and feminine roles are obvious as make-up on a poorly shaved beard, but frequently it's just two regular guys trying to understand and support each other in a world that refuses to stay regular.

The Rainbow Edition of Why Real Men Drink Straight Tequila – The Tao of Chivalry is a dear project to me. When I was a young lady, my "uncles" (One of the longest lasting couples I know to this day, by the way) were hugely impactful by being two guys who saw my inappropriate behaviors, called me on them with humor and never stopped loving me. As an example, I was arrested for selling pot in my early twenties. At the time I lived in California. When I returned to the Midwest with my tail between my legs, one of my uncles had made a little monument to my spectacular life choice and subsequent infamy. He had made a special area on his huge train diorama – Sarina's Drug Store, open 24/7. Oh! The humiliation!

Years later, I was upgraded to a ship, the SS Sarina, and redeemed when I was deserving.

During those rough years I just couldn't put anything past those two. Things other family members did not notice were obvious to the uncles. Another example: during a holiday gathering a "bullet" pipe fell out of my coat pocket and was left on their bed. If you don't know what a bullet pipe is, it is a smoking pipe that has a screw-top. It is shaped like a bullet and is small enough to fit in a coat pocket. Soooo, when the uncles found a marijuana filled bullet on their bed after they hosted a party, they knew it was mine and were patient enough to plot a humorous lesson for me. They waited until the next family gathering: mother's birthday brunch. There must have been 15 people sitting at this long table in a nice restaurant. The uncles were placed at one end of the table and I was at the other. When there was an opportune moment, one of them brought out the little pipe and loudly said, "Hey, Sarina, you left this at our place last time you came by." At which point, the pipe was passed down one side of the table, past my mother, and eventually landed at me. Clever uncles were smug as all get out, mom had no idea what she was looking at, and Sarina was humbled once again.

Clever uncles, I owe you a debt of gratitude.

Sarina Stone
www.SarinaStone.com

Eric's Introduction

———————— ❧ ————————

Eric Thurnbeck here. I've been a writing cohort of Sarina's for a while now. She was and is my teacher in the Tao, and I've got some experience of my own in counseling people about their lives and their relationships. We've become quite a team!

We had a great time writing the hetero edition of Why Real Men Drink Straight Tequila, and as the text evolved, we knew we would have to create another edition for the men who love men. As one of the members of the tribe (heyyyy girrrlll!), I knew it was a topic about which I could write with some authority.

I grew up in a small town and came of age in late 1990 early 2000. I know I had it easier than the generation before me, but the spectre of AIDS and the culture of homophobia still loomed large overhead. I got teased for being queer at school. I didn't have any gay role models. I remember it was a big deal that Doug Savant played a gay guy on Melrose Place, but even when he had boyfriends, they never got to kiss; they always just hugged and smiled at each other. Eventually I found porn, and then Queer as Folk and Will & Grace came along, but there were never any realistic portrayals of how guys actually dated each other.

Of course, as time has passed, our culture has changed. We've got a long way to go, but now being gay doesn't mean the same thing it did ten or twenty years ago.

The truth is, when we think of men, we tend to think of gay and straight men separately, barely the same species, let alone the same sex. But the principles of chivalry bind all men together, gay and straight alike – we just look at them a little bit differently.

In your hands, you hold the fruits of years of questioning, meditating, researching, and hard lessons learned through experience. In the spirit of being the change I want to see in the world, with the help of my esteemed friend, I've put to paper some of the lessons I wished were available to me when I was a younger man. I've still got lots of growing to do, but learning the way of chivalry has been a huge milestone for me.

Enjoy, gentlemen!

Eric Thurnbeck
Dude in the Tao
TheMayanViking@gmail.com

CHAPTER 1
What is This Word Tao and Why Do I See it More and More These Days?

Like all things Tao, there are interpretations of what the Chinese word "Tao" actually translates to in English. One translation is The Way of Nature. Other translations, like The Way Without Force, The Path, and The Way are also valid and correct. Understand that Chinese do not use the English alphabet nor do they think like we do. The symbols are frequently, well, more symbolic and thus lead us to feel the concept rather than form an exact picture.

What I can tell you is that Taoism is not a religion – it is a philosophy. It originated in China over 5000 years ago and was discovered by guys. Granted they were guys who shaved their heads, wore dresses, and lived in monasteries, but don't we all know a version of that? They found, through trial and error, that there are simple ways to succeed and fail in any situation. There are laws that work invisibly in all of our lives – like if you forget to put a condom in your wallet, someone fabulous will offer sex.

They discovered that the Universe is co-creating with us and all physical reality is the byproduct of our thinking. Think Keanu Reeves in the Matrix (minus the huge spike in the neck).

The problem with explaining the Tao is that it really can't be explained. What can be explained are some of the principles. If you choose to apply these principles, you will have results. These results are viewed and experienced by you exclusively, so we say your results are subjective because they are subject to your opinions and interpretation. If these results were objective they would be concrete and would be based on unemotional facts.

For example, a major principle of Taoist philosophy centers on the concept of balance. Not too much, not too little. Seems pretty simple, right? Ha!

Ever keep drinking even when you know you've had enough? Obsess over a guy you can't have? Wear pants that cut off your blood supply in an attempt to look slimmer?

These are all examples of living in a state of excess. You can't be a drama king and be a cool dude at the same time. You can't be balanced and unbalanced at the same time, either.

Balance is the way to go when making informed decisions that will lead to success and prosperity in any area, but especially when it comes to dealing with men. If relationships or romance in general cause worry and anxiety (don't lie), you're out of the game before it even starts.

The good news is that cultivating positive attitudes and belief systems can tone down, or balance, excessive negative emotions like worry and anxiety: "Intelligent, attractive men dig me." "I am my own man." "I can accomplish whatever I commit to." "No one throws me off my center." "I feel terrific tonight."

Think James Coburn in Our Man Flint.

This does not mean you just have happy, fluffy thoughts all day – that would be ridiculous (it would also be unbalanced). It means if you have an equal amount of positive and negative thoughts, you create a third element – balance – and this way of being gives you a huge advantage in your daily life, on and off the dance floor.

That was one principle. It didn't take long to explain, but it could take a lifetime to achieve.

There will be many more Taoist principles explored in this book and hopefully when you put them all together, you get a feeling for The Way of Nature, even if you can't fit the philosophy into one sentence. Once you get it, you can use it to improve your life.

Let's try another concept. Let's look at the Taoist philosophy on smiling. I know it sounds silly, but just follow me on this one. A Taoist would believe that a man will catch more flies with honey than vinegar. This exemplifies the translation The Way Without Force.

For example, you go to a pub after work to meet a few friends and there is a beautiful man sitting at the bar looking at his phone. You saunter up, order a Cosmo, and while you are waiting you turn to him and pleasantly say hello. He turns to you with a frown, says "I hate this bar," then turns away from you and stares at his phone again. Do you feel welcome? Do you want to stick around and chat? Doubtful.

Now, let's try a new scenario. You go to the same pub after work to meet your friends. There is an average looking fellow sitting at the bar. You saunter up, order a Cosmo, and while you are waiting you hear him laugh out loud. He looks up from his phone, smiles at you and says "Wanna hear something really funny?" He continues to smile as he reads you the silly joke his pal just texted him. Do you feel welcome? Do you want to stick around after your drink has been served? Maybe.

The power of a smile can change an uncomfortable silence to an invitation for interaction, and isn't that what we're looking for? Can you see how the "beautiful" man who does not smile is potentially less beautiful than the "average" man who laughs openly?

Nothing is absolute and there are always exceptions to the rule, but in general we are more attractive and inviting to other attractive and inviting people when we have a genuine smile.

You have just read about two Tao principles – Balance and The Power of a Smile. There are many more and this book will show you how you can use some of them to create satisfying, conscious relationships.

Let's get started!

More from Eric Thurnbeck on Taoism

Okay guys, so Sarina was just talking about the Tao. She mentioned the importance of balance and how living in excess can mess things up. That's just one part of the philosophy. Another really important piece is knowing that the thoughts in your head have the ability to change things around you. The simplest way I can think of to illustrate the point is this:

Think of the Force in Star Wars. It's that underlying thing that ties the universe together. It's massive and hard to understand, but we're all a part of it. We can see its laws in just about everything – gravity, the stock market, sports, and relationships.

Just like the Force, the Tao has practical applications. While it won't let you levitate, throw bolts of lightning, or wield a lightsaber, it will help you shape your life circumstances. The trick is, this will happen whether you know it or not. I've known lots of guys who put themselves in some pretty shitty situations without ever knowing how or why. On the other hand, I've known guys who set their sights on some pretty awesome things and made them happen.

Just like Luke Skywalker, you can choose to bring about the doom of the Rebel Alliance or the Empire. It all depends on what you commit to.

So the way this works is when you have a thought, your brain emits a wave of energy not unlike a radio wave; some scientists call it a "wave of possibility". When that wave touches objects or people, things start to happen on a molecular level (this is science, guys – look it up) and thus create a particle of reality. Those molecular changes, or particles, start to build up with enough waves over time. The more specific your thought is, the more specific the change. Before you know it, if you think about something long enough, it's bound to happen.

Case in point: men think about sex. We all know this. I think about sex a lot. Guys think about sex, they hang out with their buddies and talk about it, and they go out in search of it. What separates studs from losers in the sex department is the way that they think.

A stud goes out to the bar thinking, "I'm going to get laid tonight. I have guys all around me. One of these lucky boys is going home with me." Even if that guy is a smarmy douchebag, chances are pretty good he's going to score some ass, assuming he's reasonably groomed.

A loser goes out the bar thinking, "Shit, I need to get laid. I haven't been laid in forever. I wish a guy would talk to me." He's inadvertently sending men away with that kind of thinking. All he can focus on is his lack of ass, and poof, that's what he gets.

Of course, it's not enough to just think about something and expect it to happen, you actually have to do stuff too. A guy can't meditate in his house listening to Massive Attack and expect a man to show up with condoms and beer. He needs to get off his ass and go where the opportunities are.

By the same token, if a guy wants money, he needs to get a job. He's better served by sending out resumes and visualizing success than he is by buying a bunch of lottery tickets and hoping for a miracle.

The point is, you can maximize your efforts and attract opportunities to you with the correct thought patterns. Sending out the good vibrations while you're doing your thing is going to make getting what you want a hell of a lot easier. Our sex-loser at the bar is going where the boys are, but he's driving them off with negative thinking. If he sends out a different kind of wave, he's going to get a different result.

Ch. 1 What is This Word Tao and Why Do I See it More and More These Days?

Chapter 2

The Man and the Myth – Eric Debunks Social Norms

For as long as we've had language, we've told stories. Our myths have changed and grown as time has passed, but storytelling remains an enduring method of communicating.

Of course, our myths now tend to be about sexual conquests, expensive cars and clothes, the size of our cocks, and our own personal histories. Since cavemen first gathered around fires in the dark and told one another about the giant oxen they killed with spears, men have practiced the art of verbal embellishment.

We have a tendency to live according to certain stories that have been laid out for us, contributing what we can as we go along. I'm not entirely sure it's a guy thing or just a human thing, but we all like to actively participate in our own mythology.

One thing that has always interested me is how often we step into the stories that other people have crafted. It's almost like we're given a script and we blindly follow along. By buying into nebulous truths that have been around since…well, forever, we give up some of our power. When you believe these things, they become real.

Here, I'm going to address and deconstruct some of the myths about men that you may or may not have bought into. Chances are good you've heard these before.

Myth #1: Chivalry is Dead

So what is chivalry, anyway? Back in the day (and by "the day" I mean "Medieval Europe"), it was the name for the code of conduct that knights were supposed to follow. It had political, religious, and romantic aspects that were all governed under the same set of rules, most of which had to do with loyalty – to one's lord, to God, and to one's paramour. Ideally, the shining knight was a paragon of virtue, who could be counted on to fight for king, country, religion, and of course, for love. He was also expected to defend those less fortunate than himself and be a seeker of justice. At least, that's how it went in the poems and the storybooks. The reality was probably somewhat different, considering the fact that women were second-class citizens at the time, and being gay, well, that just wasn't even talked about.

Today, most people relate the idea of chivalry to men who behave like gentlemen – they're polite, respectful, and defer to the ones they're trying to woo in an effort to make them more comfortable. They're willing to court their potential mates over time, bring them flowers and gifts, hold doors open, pull out chairs, stand when they stand, throw coats over puddles, all that good stuff. Of course, a lot of that seems pretty antiquated, especially as the gender roles have been blended in the last few decades. At some point, it would seem, chivalry went out of style.

We've all heard this idea bemoaned by our girlfriends – that the knight in shining armor is a thing of the past, that men don't know how to treat women anymore. To be fair, there are some strong indicators that the ladies have a point (I'm looking at you, Jersey Shore). Sometimes, guys are dogs, and they fail to take others' feelings into account in the endless pursuit of tail.

But where does that leave us? Are we a part of the problem, or the solution? As gay men, are we supposed to be doing the wooing, and if so, can we expect to be wooed? After all, we're the ones our girlfriends come crying to when men treat them badly, but we all want our Prince Charming to show up too.

We get mixed messages these days when it comes to chivalry. Some guys want to be courted with flowers and have doors opened for them; they find it romantic. Others take offense at the idea that they can't open the doors for themselves, and equate gentlemanly gestures with some kind of hidden agenda. Still others would rather dispense with the flowers altogether, and just crack open a beer instead. As a result, lots of men are left jumping from one foot to the next, trying to navigate that tricky line between Upstanding Guy and Insensitive Ass.

It's no wonder that we all have conflicting ideas about chivalry – not many people can agree on what it means, whether or not it still exists, or if it's even important. At the end of the day, though, everyone wants to be treated well, so why shouldn't we strive toward good conduct?

For lots of guys, the ideals are just annoying to try to live up to. The real irony is that while we all secretly hope for Mr. Right to show up, too often we get caught in the trap of not being Mr. Right, so everybody gets left waiting. We resent it when men don't expend the effort to make us feel special. Those who do try resent it when their gestures go unacknowledged, or worse, when they try to be chivalrous and then get their hearts broken.

I've known lots of guys who were hesitant to pull out all the romantic stops because when they did so in the past, their partners became demanding and expectant of constant adoration. It became unrealistic and exhausting to sustain, so they stopped trying.

While understandable, this inevitably fuels the perception that men will only really strive for romance when relationships are new, leading all of us to become bitter and skeptical of gestures delivered in good faith.

Clearly, living out this myth is less than satisfying for all parties involved.

Another problem comes with the fact that our model for chivalry is all wrapped up in the idea of the shining knight and the damsel in distress – between two guys, who's who? If two knights come together, do they swordfight to see who gets to rescue who? (Come to think of it, that sounds fun ...) Do the rules that apply to men and women apply to men who date other men? We've kind of had to make our own rules as we go along, and in many cases, what we were taught about gender roles growing up becomes somewhat obsolete when we're adults. As often as we try to categorize one another as either butch or femme, we have to acknowledge that it's rarely so simple. The Yin/Yang balance of a relationship (more on that later) is quite likely to shift based on circumstances and interpersonal chemistry, so truth be told, we usually get to take turns being the guy in our relationships. That means both men have to be aware of the chivalric ideal and be ready to live up to their end of the bargain when duty calls. This is a tall order, especially when many gay men don't buy into the idea that chivalry applies to them.

I would counter that for us, chivalry just needs to be framed differently. Everybody wants to be with people they feel supported by, and while the rules that applied hundreds of years ago to men and women don't all still carry the same weight, the need for loyalty and appreciation is still there. As human consciousness has changed, so have the meanings of the words we've used to define it.

Could chivalry be reinvented? Could it go through rehab and make a comeback, like Robert Downy Jr. did? I'm inclined to think so, if it's stripped down to something everybody can use. We can't fall back on the old definitions, because to make them apply to us, they have to morph into something new.

But what the hell does that look like?

Honestly, we have a tendency to overthink this. In my opinion, chivalry can really be boiled down to two simple ideals: living by the Golden Rule, and having a clear picture in your mind of what you want to see in a man. Is he honest? Brave? Does he put the toilet seat down? Does he like holding hands in public? Will he comfort you when you cry? Is he diligent about flossing?

We've all made wish lists about the perfect guy and tucked them away in our hope chests, and that's great, but that's only the first part of getting your wondrously chivalrous mate. The trick to sealing the deal is this: once you've pictured your dream-dude clearly in your mind and you understand exactly what he needs to be to make you happy – modify your behavior to be that guy. You will be astounded at the caliber of men you attract when you start modeling the behavior you'd like to see in others. You know that quote about being the change you want to see in the world? Yeah, that applies to your love life.

Some points to consider:

- The values of loyalty and appreciation are the true core of the ideal of chivalry. You don't have to ride a white horse and rescue distressed dudes from burning buildings, but you can't be a lying greedy douche and still say you're chivalrous.

- You have no business asking others to be loyal and appreciative of you if you are disloyal and dismissive to them. Be ready to give what you're hoping to get in return.

- You're not the only guy in the relationship, so the loyalty and appreciation should go both ways. Don't waste your best material on men who don't deserve it. A guy who can't deign to say "thank you" (and mean it) when you make a gesture or give a gift is no prize at all. Therefore, it's not ungentlemanly to walk away.

- Chivalry isn't a script to be followed; it's not a formula or an equation. It has to be expressed authentically and individually. Just because another guy did something for a lover and got awesome results, that doesn't mean it'll work for you. Find ways of expressing the ideal that feels natural to you – after all, confidence is sexy, and you don't want to use moves that make you look awkward.

- That said, chivalry also has to be individualized to the recipient. Meaning, if you're going to make a guy a playlist, find out what kind of music he likes instead of just giving him your favorite songs and hoping he'll think you're awesome. If he has no use for flowers but likes gadgets, get him a data storage device or new software instead. And for crap's sake, if he's vegan, don't take him to an expensive steak joint. If you want to make your man feel appreciated, it makes sense to use gestures he'll actually appreciate.

This stuff sounds simple, guys, but I've personally seen many friends of mine screw up all of these things and wonder why their love lives sucked. I'd bet money that most of you have too.

The bottom line is this: chivalry's not dead; it's just different now than it was before. If we quit trying to buy into a set of rules that stopped being relevant centuries ago and start manning up and living in the now, being the guys we want to be with, we stand a much better chance of hitting the goals we've set for ourselves. If you act like the man your dream-dude would want to date, you won't have to piss and moan about why he's not with you.

Myth #2: Nice Guys Finish Last

You're at the bar. You're hanging out with your friends; you're a bunch of reasonably quirky, cool guys. You're funny. You tell great stories. Even if you can't dance worth a shit, you're probably endearing. Maybe you need to hit the gym, (if only those last few inches would just disappear!) but you're not a hideous freak of nature. You're not poor, but you're not rich.

You are, in short, most of the guys in the free world.

And then, over there, those guys are sitting on the bar's leather couch, surrounded by beautiful boys. They're the Glitterati. They've got perfect teeth. Their hair is the effortless combination of bed-head and style, and you can spot an Abercrombie logo from over here. They're charming. They're witty. They're smooth. You'd bet money that at least one of them has syphilis.

They are, in short, the obnoxiously gorgeous assholes that those beautiful boys are going home with.

It's very easy to fall into the trap of envying what other guys have. We're men, after all, and competition is practically hardwired into our DNA (more on that later). That being said, my entire life I've heard it said that to get ahead in this world, you have to be willing to step over others, to grab life by the balls and take what you want from it. Ambition is a trait to be respected, and passivity (or worse, ugh, niceness) is one to be mocked and avoided.

In this world, wealth and six-pack abs reign supreme. That being the case, it becomes very tempting to give in to the impulse to act like a dick to get what you want. We're all dicks sometimes, but with some guys, it becomes a habit, and then the habit becomes a pattern.

The sad truth is, shitty behavior is rewarded more often than it should be, and all the nice guys in the world are left shaking their heads in dismay while the lowlife bastards make all the money and have all the hot sex.

The belief in this myth plays out in many different ways. One of the most common I've seen is when a guy is into a friend he's known forever but the friend's in love with some useless tit who's either a paragon that drives a nice car or a parasite that spends all of his money. The nice guy in the scenario probably chews his nails and drowns his sorrow in beer while trying to play the good friend, comforting his buddy when his asshole boyfriend makes him cry ("Oh, I don't know what I'd do without you!" he says). He may eventually break down and tell his friend how he feels, only to be utterly humiliated ("Oh wow, I love you so much, but you're like a brother to me!"). It's easy to see how that can lead a dude to become bitter and come to the conclusion that being sweet gets you nowhere and being a jerkoff gets you laid.

There's a trick to this, though, guys – the smug satisfaction on that asshole's face is an illusion. Men who constantly take what they want without any consideration for others might look like they have it all, but the reality is that none of it lasts. Whenever men have to resort to shady means to get ahead, it creates a nightmare of red tape behind the scenes.

In the I Ching (a totally smart book that was written in China over 2,000 years ago) there's a passage called The Army. The long and short of it is to have a winning army, you need a good general. If the general acts like a prick to get to the top, he's eventually going to lose the loyalty and support of his soldiers'. Think about it – a guy who has a history of screwing others over isn't going to have many people to ask for favors when he's up against a wall. It's only a matter of time before wronged parties from the past come calling, and it'll be hard for him to make a hasty retreat when he's burned all of his bridges.

The other sucky part about constantly stepping over others to get what you want is that 99% of the time, you're being driven by the ego. I know guys, the ego kinda rocks sometimes, but the truth is, it's a pain in the ass. The ego is a lot like an incessantly needy, demanding boyfriend who always wants you to buy him stuff. As soon as you give in and give it what it wants, the ego says great, good job, you're a badass – now do this even bigger thing to prove you're more of a badass. Any of you who've ever blown a paycheck (or two, or twenty) on a guy who could never be satisfied knows exactly what I'm talking about. And just like that guy who feeds on your money, the ego feeds on your anxiety and leads you into more and more dickish behavior.

So, what does that say about the rest of us who look at guys like that and think, damn, I want what he has? Really, guys, it just says we're insecure and we're not happy with our lives. If you feel envious, anxious, and threatened most of the time, what kind of life are you really living? Even moments of glory will feel short-lived, and you'll miss out on the satisfaction they might otherwise bring. And when you feel like you have something to defend or to prove, it makes it really easy to resort to terrible measures to reach your goal.

So what do we do to change that?

The first thing you have to accept is this – if you buy into the idea that being kind puts you at the bottom of the food chain, that makes it true. Not only will you rationalize victimizing others to move up the ladder, you'll attract the unwelcome attention of other guys willing to do the same thing to you. You then get locked into this dog-eat-dog mentality that's really hard to break out of, because it's constantly reinforced.

Envy isn't an acceptable reason to chuck your morals out the window – it's a big sign that you need to check yourself. You have to be willing to step outside the reality you've built and make a conscious choice to change it. In layman's terms, you have to give yourself an attitude adjustment and tell yourself it's not okay to be an asshole.

Some points to consider:

- Being nice doesn't equate to being a doormat. It's perfectly fine to stick up for yourself, especially if someone's treating you like shit. You don't have to resort to being a jackass; being assertive does the trick nicely. Keep your spine intact while you adjust your attitude.

- Similarly, being boring doesn't make you nice. You don't have to sacrifice what makes you who you are to fit other people's molds of what good behavior looks like. It's really a simple matter of being courteous, respectful, and considerate of the people around you. Don't just shut down to avoid offending people – get involved in a way that's constructive.

- Being a dick doesn't make you cool. It makes you a dick. It doesn't earn you respect; it earns you animosity and resentment. As you know, nothing's quite as satisfying as seeing a dick get what he's got coming to him. Don't be that guy.

- While it's true that the objects of our affection are often attracted to jerks, that's not a reason to adopt a jerk persona just to score tail. The truth is, you don't really want those guys. Let the jerks have them, and focus on winning someone who'll appreciate the nice guy you are. Men who dig assholes have issues of their own, and there's no point in making their issues yours.

While you may be having flashbacks to kindergarten while reading this, it's amazing how often grown men need to be reminded of how to play nice with others.

The bottom line is, you'll attract men of a whole different caliber if you can display genuine kindness when it's called for. Sincerity is what separates the men who get chased from the rest of the herd, and it has the awesome side effect of feeling good too. Instead of worrying about finishing last, learn to believe that nice guys finish best, and they certainly laugh the longest.

Myth #3: Men Only Want One Thing

Okay, so to be fair, there's a grain of truth to this one.

Saying that men want sex is a little bit like saying water is wet. It's something of a foregone conclusion among most adults. Everybody knows that men like to get laid, and that sometimes they can be cavalier about it.

However, while a man's sexual drive is nothing to scoff at, to say that sex is the only thing driving him is more than a little simplistic.

This belief is a bit of a chicken-or-egg scenario – are men thought to be insatiable horndogs because they behave that way? Or do they behave that way because everyone thinks they're supposed to? It's of course true that there are exceptions to the stereotype, though guys who fall outside the horndog norm are looked at a little strangely – What's wrong with that guy? The idea of a man without a sex drive is kind of like a car without wheels: the frame is there, you can recognize if for what it is, but it's not going to get you where you need to go.

Among straight men, sexual prowess is widely considered a measure of manhood. With gay men, this is partially true, but sexual desirability is a much bigger status symbol. It doesn't hurt if your cock is huge, either. Interestingly, our straight brothers will exaggerate and outright lie to their peers to impress them with tales of their sexual conquest, but for us, being seen as a stud by our friends is much less important than being seen as one by our potential mates. We want to be liked, of course, but we also want to be wanted. This leads us to play up our physical attributes as much as possible, strutting like peacocks to gather admirers. It's less about how good we are in the sack and more about how many guys want to get us there.

The belief that sex is all that matters to us is easy to buy into, because lots of us lead with our dicks (I know that mine has made more than one stupid decision on my behalf). This can make it difficult to shift gears when sex stops being about casual fun and starts being about intimacy. However, just because getting off is the first thing on our minds (in most cases), that doesn't mean it's the only thing. But if you don't stick around long enough to let a guy get to know you beyond the initial tumble, he's going to assume that's all you're really interested in.

So what's really going on behind all the posturing? Are gay men single-minded Neanderthals who only think as far as their next orgasm and can't ever find relationships? Hardly. The truth is, sex might be easy, but intimacy presents more of a challenge.

Here's the kicker, though, guys – men want to have relationships just as much as they like to have sex. Men wouldn't embroil themselves in all the drama of love if sex was all they were getting out of it. After all, sex isn't that hard to find when it comes down to it, as anyone with Grindr or Scruff can tell you. But guys willingly subject themselves to all kinds of heavy lifting, late-night phone calls, arguments via text, and "what are you thinking about?" conversations just to be near the objects of their… lust? I don't think so. I've never seen a man break down and cry because a guy wouldn't sleep with him, but I have seen that happen when one wouldn't love him.

In my experience, when gay men meet, attraction (or lack thereof) tends to make itself known pretty quickly, and with no one around to say no, it's easy to tumble into bed without getting a good sense of who it is we're screwing. This is all well and good, but when it causes us to view each other as endlessly replaceable, it diminishes the value of making a sexy, intimate connection with someone who might bring lasting value to our life, be it as a friend, lover, or romantic partner. How that person contributes to your experience can look like a million different things, and there's no one right way to do it.

It's important to remember this – whether you know the guy you're getting naked with for an hour or a decade, he's a person who wants things beyond the throbbing hard-on you're letting him play with. That said, remember your manners, and think about the story he's going to tell his friends tomorrow – is it going to be about a hot hookup with this great guy he met, or will it be a cautionary tale about an asshole he couldn't get away from fast enough?

Some points to consider:

- If you act like sex is all that matters to you, guys are going to think that sex is all that matters to you. Sure, it's fun to be a dog, but that's going to earn you a dog's reputation. There's no need to abandon the fun sexy time altogether, but let your interests and unique characteristics be known, and let yourself shine through even if you're just hooking up. Acting in the fullness of yourself is going to make it much more likely you'll attract the right kind of partners.

- Conversely, if a guy treats you like you're an asshole or makes you feel guilty for wanting to have sex with him (and you're not being an asshole about it), you might want to take a step back and ask what's really going on here. If he's trying to abuse your sexual dynamic to have control of the relationship, pull up your stakes and get out of there. Nobody deserves to be extorted. It doesn't matter if he's hot, that kind of behavior is creepy and pathological.

- The idea that you're only supposed to think with your dick is someone else's idea. All the posturing in the world won't make it true. Even the biggest cock hound likes the idea of waking up next to someone and just appreciating him being there. Don't play into someone else's script if it keeps you from what you want.

- Don't place judgments on yourself for liking sex and expressing yourself sexually. It's a fun, hot, natural way for you to connect with others, and as long as you're healthy and aware about it, there's no reason to repress yourself. That said, remember that living in excess isn't healthy either – if your sexual self is all you're expressing, you and the people around you are missing out. Even flaws could be sexy to the right guy, so let your freak flag fly and enjoy everything you (and they) have to offer.

Well guys, there you have it. Of course, these aren't the only myths about men that people believe in; they're just the most common in my experience. Just remember, any time you buy into some vague truth about a large group of people, there's a big chance you're missing something. Be willing to look past appearances and ask questions. The answers just might surprise you.

And knowing the truth makes it a hell of a lot easier to shape your world into what you want it to be.

CHAPTER 3

Who Cares If I Get Along With My Mother? (Where Does Failure and Fear of Rejection Come From?)

Hey guys, Sarina here.

There's this saying in the profession of psychology: "What we resist, persists." It makes sense when you understand the effect of brainwaves on pretty much everything. If you want to know what you believe to be true about money, sex, love, health, and life in general, just take a look at your life.

Once you accept that your Universe is a projection of your belief system, you live with two questions:

1. How do I hold a vision of my dream life long and strong enough to make it happen?

2. What do I want?

The second question is tricky because what we want can be confused with what we expect. Here's an example:

I have a few friends who take jobs at resorts every summer. One fellow, we'll call him Dexter, has regaled us with tales of how he loses a boyfriend each year he takes this job. Dexter has identified his temporary job with that outcome. According to him, he has been victimized and scarred by repeated abandonment.

At one point, before leaving the city to take this illustrious job, this man hooked up with a very sweet boy and they became a couple. Although he lived a half-day drive from his job, that summer the new boy, having fallen in love with Dexter, made himself available in every way. He flatly told Dexter that all he wanted was to be together, and he didn't give a shit about the logistics. Oh, and he never said no to sex – bonus!

Before Dexter left for this job, he encouraged his new boy to make plans to visit him as he was very excited to share this experience. We all thought Dexter's bad luck had come to an end.

Here's what Dexter did next…

He became unromantic and started treating the boy badly; really badly. We all saw it and could not believe it.

This is a perfect illustration of the lengths to which people go to keep their stories alive. When Dexter's boyfriend did not abandon him like he expected, he jumped through flaming hoops to make abandonment happen.

Oh, just for the record, when being an ass did not work, he dumped the sweet boy. Bravo Dexter!

This chapter is about how our subconscious thoughts run our lives. This is where the question, "Who cares if I get along with my mother?" comes into play.

The first thing you have to know in order to take control of your subconscious is basic brain physiology.

Your brain connects thoughts through channels called neural pathways. These paths interconnect to hundreds of other pathways that lead to all of your functions and thoughts. They tell your body to move and your organs to work. They connect your feelings to your memories. They lead to vital thoughts like the date of Pride and which guys have great abs.

Think of thoughts as rooms in your brain. When we use a neural pathway leading to a specific room, we strengthen not only that room and pathway, but also its connection to other thoughts and belief rooms.

It gets really crazy when you realize that your brain does not know the difference between what it is experiencing right now and what it remembers.

When it comes to relating to men, you have to accept that their mothers were the first people most of us learned to trust. Thoughts about mom created a belief. If she was delightful and perfect, you got lucky. You just burned a neuropathway to the happy room. You get fed, you get cared for, and life is good.

If she was less than stable, or rejected you in some way, welcome to the unhappy dysfunctional room! You learned that love and safety come with nasty strings attached.

It is not silly to take a look at your current attitudes about love and life in general. It is not a waste of time to compare your childhood experiences and beliefs to your current experiences and beliefs.

The successful man does not accept victimization as a way of life.

If you are delighted with your current state of affairs, then leave things alone. If it ain't broke, don't fix it.

Like Tim Robbins in The Shawshank Redemption, the successful man in the new millennium digs a tunnel out of prison to freedom. Sure you can wait for an outside source (in the film it was the Parole Board) to set you free, like Morgan Freeman did. But it'll take a lot longer and it's not a sure thing.

It takes balls to admit that you have created something that sucks, and even more to want to dig your way out.

If there's a tunnel that leads you back to prison, you have to stop using it. If you keep digging long enough in the right direction, the prison will collapse behind you just because you're not there.

The bad experiences in your childhood can affect you in a few ways:

1. You might repeat the behavior you didn't like with other people, doing to them what was done to you.

2. You might seek out people to do the same bad things to you over and over (crazy, but more common than you'd think).

3. If you're really awesome and aware, you will swear that will never happen again in your life, ever. Like Jean Luc Picard, you make it so.

If you want to be the guy in scenario #3, then you must replace the old dysfunctional beliefs with new successful ones.

Oh, the beer chaser to this is that not only do we create pathways of behavior, but we also become addicted to the chemicals they produce. Yes, you can become an addict to the chemicals certain situations or emotions generate. Think Vin Diesel in XXX. It took a lot of adrenalin to get him off, so he became extreme over time. Extremely sexy, but extreme just the same.

The good news is that you are capable of generating all those awesome chemicals through positive behaviors, too. You can be a junkie without hurting yourself or anyone else. You can fall in love and release doses of Oxytocin (a wonderful hormone) in to your system. You can create wonderful scenarios with men that generate adrenaline (a hormone and neurotransmitter). Bottom line, you can become aware of your brain and body and have as peaceful or wild of an experience as you desire.

Remember that.

Ch. 3 Who Cares If I Get Along With My Mother?

CHAPTER 4

Elements of Masculinity

Brief introduction from Sarina

Now that you have a little background on what Taoism is and how your thoughts create your physical reality, we're going to go forward and start using these ideas to make good things happen in your life. In this chapter, we focus on a major Taoist principle: The Elements of nature.

My esteemed co-author, Eric Thurnbeck, has painstakingly created one of the coolest explanations for not only understanding why the Elements of nature apply to your life, but also how to use them to get what you want.

It took a lot of work, but I think this may be one of the user-friendliest guides to using the Taoist Elemental Principle I've ever seen. You will need to practice, but once you understand how each Element either creates or destroys another Element, you can use the technology to guide most social situations.

To be fair, I should warn you that any technology can be used or abused and this is no exception. It should be used to transform negative situations in to positive and help you attain your goals.

I trust you to be chivalrous gentlemen and not take advantage.

Without further ado, Eric Thurnbeck.

Elements of Masculinity

There are two concepts that are basic, fundamental aspects of Taoist thought: Yin and Yang, and the five Elements. You've probably heard of Yin and Yang. The Elements might be new to you, and they're a little different than the four Greek Elements we're used to in the West. In any case, these ideas are the foundations of many Taoist practices, which in turn helped inspire this book.

The cool part is, you're probably already using some of what I'm about to tell you, though you may not be conscious of it. Take a closer look with me and you'll see what I mean.

Yin and Yang

Let's talk about Yin and Yang first, because everything else will fall under that concept. Yin and Yang describe a wholeness that is achieved through the balance of opposites. Light and dark, hot and cold, male and female – these are all examples of Yin and Yang in action, but they don't describe the whole idea.

Yang is the active, creative principle of the universe; it's what makes stuff happen. Yin is the passive, receptive principle of the universe; it's what lets stuff happen.

An easy way to think about it is a field goal in football – the kicker who sends the football flying through the air is the Yang principle. The space between the goalposts is the Yin principle. When they meet, the team scores.

Yin is a bottom. Yang is a top. It's that union and duality that makes the whole universe work. One side can't do its thing without the other.

Yang – Making an impact

Yang is what many guys aspire to naturally – not surprising, since Yang is thought of as a powerfully masculine force, though men don't have a monopoly on it. Yang is dynamite and explosions, bursts of energy, it's heat, it's drive and speed, inspiration, passion, and potency – pretty much everything that leaves an impression on its surroundings.

So what does Yang look like in practice? Basically any time you're changing your environment through action – whether you're doing something as simple as starting a conversation or as complex as inspiring a political movement – you're invoking Yang energy. The example I think of for Yang is an old macho standby, Agent 007, James Bond. He knocks men out with a single punch, he blows stuff up, he drives fast cars and beds hot women – Bond on the move is quintessential Yang.

Of course, Yang is an energy that's impossible to maintain indefinitely; it just burns up too much fuel. Knowing when to bust out with Yang requires some finesse and sensitivity – if you use it too often, it loses its potency, and then you have to raise the bar to make an impact.

So when should you whip out your Yang? Consider the following:

- Is decisive action needed to produce an immediate result?
- Are you stuck in a rut and does something need to change?
- Are you trying to inspire change in others?
- Have the other parties in the situation taken a passive role?
- Are you trying to create something new?

If the answer to the appropriate question is yes, Yang may be the best approach. These are only a few possible scenarios, but I've kept them vague so they can apply in lots of situations. Use your judgment, but the rule I use is, if I see something isn't going to naturally happen on its own, I might help nudge it along by being more active.

For example:

Let's say you're sitting in a team meeting, listening to your boss give a presentation. The material is less than fascinating. Your boss is trying to get some participation, but it's like that scene in Ferris Bueller's Day Off where Ben Stein is calling out, "Bueller? Bueller?" and everyone is just sort of staring at the poor guy.

- You could just sit there, hoping to avoid looking dumb or like a kiss-ass and just not say anything. With any luck, your boss won't call on you. That would be taking a passive approach, or invoking Yin.

- On the other hand, you could throw your boss a bone and respond to one of the questions he's asked, or make a smart, relevant comment about the material. That would be taking an active approach, or invoking Yang.

Just remember, guys, Yang is a force to be used carefully. When it gets out of control, people end up with hangovers, black eyes, bruised egos, STDs and criminal records. That said, without it, nothing exciting ever happens!

Yin – Playing it cool

Yin is the complement to the explosive energy of Yang – it's cool, receptive, quiet, still, and passive. Yin is the calm after a storm, the silence of an empty room, a blank page, an empty beer stein, and the bed that's waiting for you at the end of a long day. While Yin is traditionally regarded as feminine, its energy is present in both men and women.

So how does Yin show up in people's behavior? It's pretty simple really. Any time you opt to wait something out, or achieve a result without action – whether you're biding your time at the DMV or letting someone else make an ass of himself by keeping your mouth shut – you're invoking Yin energy.

Many guys might think Yin is too wimpy for their tastes; they might even regard it as cowardly or unmanly. Yin might look weak on the surface, but the truth is there's an enormous wellspring of power that comes from it. What they say about still waters running deep is absolutely true, and the ability to harness the power of Yin can turn you into a Crouching Tiger/Hidden Badass.

Like Yang, the example I use to demonstrate the power of Yin is 007, James Bond. Yeah, he blows stuff up and beats guys to a pulp and drives fast cars, but he is at his absolute coolest when he stands stock-still, dry martini in hand and leaning against the bar, just watching the room and assessing the situation. He's tall, he's awesome, he's wearing a tuxedo, and he's not doing anything. But somehow, that's always when the beautiful Bond girls show up. Bond has the perfect balance of Yin and Yang, which makes him pretty friggin fantastic.

When is the Yin approach most effective? Consider the following:

- Does the situation allow for pause before action?
- Are there lots of conflicting or unexplained variables present?
- Are the consequences of acting rashly greater than those of waiting?
- Are you trying to inspire self-sufficiency in others?
- Have the other parties in the situation taken an active role?

If the answer to the appropriate question is yes, then Yin is probably the best approach. Truth be told, unless decisive action is needed right then, I almost always default to Yin first – it's really just a good way to hedge your bets. If you're not a patient person, this will probably be tough to pull off, but it's certainly worth the practice.

For example:

Let's say some bitchy queen is getting in your face because he thinks you cut in front of him in line at the bar. He's talking loudly and making some rude comments, clearly trying to bait you into starting a slap-fight or something. You can tell he's probably had more than his limit, and people are starting to turn and stare, waiting to see some drama.

- You could get back in the guy's face and ask him what the hell his problem is, engaging him in the conflict. Given the presence of alcohol in both your bloodstreams, this might result in a disco-brawl, getting both of you bounced. This would be taking an active approach, or invoking Yang.
- On the other hand, you could coolly ignore the guy, share a knowing look with the bartender without saying anything, take your drinks, and leave. If he keeps it up, chances are good he'll get bounced without you having to lift a finger. This would be taking a passive approach, or invoking Yin.

The downside to Yin is that when it's relied upon too often, stagnation sets in. If you're always waiting to see what's going to happen, eventually nothing will – and then your only option is to kick yourself in the ass to get the ball rolling. The key to mastering this is knowing when to wait and when to act – there's no hard-and-fast formula; it just takes practice and good judgment on your part. People, being people, always screw it up from time to time, but if you can eventually be right more often than you're wrong, you'll be in good shape and your life circumstances will show it.

The Five Elements

The five Chinese Elements are Fire, Earth, Metal, Water, and Wood. In the West, we're used to the Greek Elements of Earth, Air, Fire, and Water. That cosmology is very wrapped up in what the Element is. The Chinese way of thought has a lot more to do with what the Element does.

According to Taoist philosophy, the Elements are not metaphors used to describe different mindsets or states of being, rather Elements are literally contained within our body and psyche and should be controlled.

Each Element has positive and negative emotional associations, shown below:

Element	Positive Emotion	Negative Emotion
Fire	Love	Hatred/Cruelty
Earth	Openness	Worry/Anxiety
Metal	Courage/Righteousness	Sorrow/Depression
Water	Gentleness	Fear
Wood	Kindness	Anger

The Elements work in a cycle – Fire burns and creates Earth, Earth compresses and produces Metal, Metal cools and condenses Water, Water flows and nourishes Wood, Wood grows and fuels Fire. That cycle can also become destructive: Fire burns and melts Metal, Metal is sharpened and cuts Wood, Wood grows roots and depletes Earth, Earth is built and dams Water, Water flows and douses Fire.

The cycle looks like this:

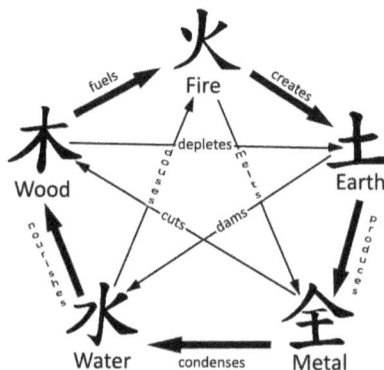

The practice of using the elemental cycles to produce results or changes in behavior is referred to as inner alchemy. Smart Chinese guys have been using inner alchemy for literally thousands of years to practice medicine and to improve their lives. When practicing inner alchemy, the goal is usually to generate positive emotions or situations from negative ones. Generating negative emotions on purpose, while possible, is kind of a dick thing to do (and it will likely inspire others to do it to you).

I think of the Elements as building blocks or tools and inner alchemy as the vehicle to creation. Just as you need the right tools to fix certain things, you need the right Elements to create and respond to certain situations.

I'm sure it all sounds very Captain Planet, but it'll make more sense once we go into each one.

Fire – Forging ahead

All the guys I know like to play with Fire – I'm pretty sure most of us were budding pyromaniacs when we were kids. Fire is awesome, and there's a certain caveman satisfaction that comes with lighting and controlling it (as anyone who's ever successfully built a campfire can tell you). And people who can control it without getting burned, like the hot fire fighters we see in calendars and porn, generally impress the rest of us.

Fire has three properties that tell us how it works on an energetic level:

- Fire generates heat
- Fire sheds light, drawing attention to itself
- Fire has to consume fuel in order to exist

Fire is associated with the color red, the positive emotion of Love and the negative emotions of Hatred and Cruelty. All of those feelings are like Fire in that they seem to burn when we feel them – sometimes they're experienced as physical pain. Have you ever "seen red" when you hated someone? People with heavy Fire certainly draw attention to themselves; it's pretty obvious when someone's in the throes of Love or Hate. And both Love and Hatred have to be fed in order to exist – without fuel, they tend to sputter out into a mild fondness or distaste, and eventually into indifference.

People with lots of Fire tend to be loud, energetic, boisterous, passionate, and intense. Those without enough of it tend to be quiet, withdrawn, and to be honest, kinda boring. Too much can be just as bad as too little, though – if you've ever been around someone who sucked up all the air in the room and made you tired just by being there, you know what I mean.

A good example of how Fire looks in a man is Ewan McGregor's portrayal of Christian in the 2001 musical, Moulin Rouge! As is pointed out numerous times, he has a ridiculous obsession with Love, and he is a constant draw for attention due to his musical and lyrical talent. When his flame burns bright, he is vibrant and colorful, but when it burns out, he becomes despondent, heartbroken, and gray. In the film's climax, we see the other side of Fire when he reacts with Cruelty after being rejected by the woman he loves.

So how can Fire be used?

Of all the elements, Fire is probably the most obvious in its application – the results tend to be both visible and immediate. When a man invokes Fire, he becomes more obvious and attention-grabbing – Love and Hate are really powerful; by their nature, they're hard to do half-assed.

In the cycle of Elements, Fire creates Earth and overcomes Metal. That means Love (Fire) can create Openness (Earth) or overcome Sorrow (Metal). Applying the negative emotions, Hatred or Cruelty (Fire) can create Worry or Anxiety (Earth) or overcome Courage or Righteousness (Metal). While the negative emotions can sometimes be used to overcome other negative emotions, this should be done with the utmost caution and sincerity. Obviously, using negative emotions to intentionally generate more negative emotions is just silly, so don't do it.

For example:

Fire creating Earth – Let's say your guy has been acting a little distant lately, kinda closed off and fidgety. He says everything's fine when you ask him what's the matter, but you can tell he seems to be anxious about something. You want to try to fix it, but you've got to know what's wrong first. You need him to be Open. Knowing that Openness is the positive attribute of the Earth element, you can choose to bust out with Fire to get him to open up.

- The positive emotion of Fire is Love – ratcheting up the Fire could involve verbalizing your feelings more frequently (the words "I love you" possess near-magical properties when spoken out loud), touching him lovingly more often (not just when you want nookie), and in general just finding ways to ensure he has no reason to doubt your Love for him. With any luck, this will grow the Openness he needs to feel to tell you what's up.

- The other side of Fire is Hatred – if the situation has deteriorated enough, you may consider honestly letting him know that you hate the fact that he's pulled away and you really wish he'd tell you what was wrong so you could help. You've got to back that up with Love too, though, or you could make the situation even worse.

Fire overcoming Metal – Let's say a good buddy of yours has been moping around for a while now after having been disappointed in love. At first you were sympathetic and supportive, then patient, then annoyed, and now worried. He's clearly depressed, and enough time has passed that he should have snapped out of it. Knowing that Sorrow is the negative expression of Metal, you can use Fire to overcome it.

- Sometimes our friends need to be reminded that they're lovable. Be generous with your displays of affection and be present as much as possible. Making yourself vulnerable and having a sincere conversation about what he's feeling might help him get his shit together – at the very least he'll be aware that his behavior is making his friends worry, which might prompt him to do something about it.

- On the other hand, sometimes some tough Love is in order. The other side of Fire is Cruelty – while it absolutely must be used sparingly and appropriately, there's no denying it produces results. You may just have to tell your bro to get his ass off the couch and into the shower to rejoin the world of the living, whether he likes it or not. Just make sure you're coming from a place of Love, and that you've tried the nice approach first (the scene where Seth Rogen flicks Paul Rudd in the nuts near the end of The 40 Year Old Virgin is a masterful example of this very scenario).

Some final tips about playing with Fire:

- Fire is rarely subtle. Choosing to act with it usually means that others will notice what you're doing. If that's what you're going for, this is a bonus.

- Fire is dynamic and alluring. Those who display it a lot are often the center of attention. This can be really heady and tempting to indulge. Enjoy your time in the spotlight, but be willing to step out of it when the time comes.

- Fire needs fuel to burn. You'll quickly figure out how tiring it is to be dynamic all the time – if you're going full throttle non-stop, you'll eventually hit a wall and crash hard. Moderate to a slow burn, and you can go much farther.

- Fire can nurture the Fire in others. By serving as a positive example of a man who can live and Love with pride and integrity, you can encourage others to do the same. That will make you the kind of man other men want to be.

Earth – Staying grounded

Like Fire, guys like to play with Earth as kids, digging in the dirt, building dams and tunnels, getting mud all over the place. I was sort of an indoor child, but even I liked going outside and getting dirty now and then. Guys who work in or with the earth, like gardeners, landscapers, and miners, are thought of as "salt of the earth" type guys, the kind who seal a deal with a handshake.

Earth has three properties that tell us how it works energetically:

- Earth is inert and neutral, providing common ground for all
- Earth can be mined for its resources, such as metals and nutrients
- Earth is stable, solid, predictable, and provides our foundation for living

Earth is associated with the color yellow, the positive emotion of Openness, and the negative emotions of Worry and Anxiety. These feelings are like earth for several reasons – most importantly that they serve as foundations for ways of life. Those who live openly and honestly enjoy lives of comfort and predictability, while those who worry and fret constantly are always on shaky ground. These emotions can also yield other feelings; Openness provides many opportunities for growth, and Anxiety can be turned into powerful motivation as long as it's not paralyzing.

People who exemplify Earth tend to be pretty stable; others describe them as "well grounded" and "down to earth". They're usually straightforward, not many frills or pretensions, and are practical problem solvers. An overload of Earth might make someone a bit too grounded, lacking spontaneity, or they might be too Open and honest, not filtering thoughts they should leave private (and they usually won't see why people get so offended when they speak them out loud – we've all known that guy). Conversely, those without much Earth seem ungrounded and unstable, unpredictable, flighty, and directionless.

An unusual but potent example of the Earth Element in film can be found in the late Patrick Swayze's portrayal of Vida Boheme in 1995's To Wong Foo, Thanks for Everything! Julie Newmar. Vida's choices are driven by a strong desire for Openness (both from herself and from others), but are equally influenced by her perpetual Worry and Anxiety about how others will receive her. When the film reaches its conclusion, she has found solid ground and becomes Open to the future and frees herself from her painful past.

So how can Earth be used?

Earth tends to be way mellower than Fire in its application. When Earth is brought to the table in a positive way, it usually takes things down a notch and brings people together. Openness makes it cool for everyone to lay their stuff on the table without fear of being judged.

In the cycle of Elements, Earth creates Metal and overcomes Water. That means Openness (Earth) can create Courage or Righteousness (Metal) or overcome Fear (Water). Applying the negative emotions, Worry or Anxiety (Earth) can create Sorrow (Metal) or overcome Gentleness (Water). As with Fire, negative emotions can overcome other negative emotions, but this requires savvy and sincerity to make it work.

For example:

Earth creating Metal – Let's say a lady friend of yours has a really crappy, toxic relationship with her mom. Once again, she's called you in tears because her hydra of a mother has undermined her sense of self-worth. Are you going to let this awesome chick get down on herself because her mom's a bitch? Hell no! You know she needs to be brave and Righteous so she can stand up for herself, which is the province of the Metal Element. Earth will help grow the Metal and change the situation.

- In this instance, you can express your Openness by just being honest and frank about what you think of your friend and how she's being treated. Share what you've seen and thought about her and her mom. Be Open about the fact that she deserves to be treated better – the idea is to build the Righteousness she'll need to grow a lady-set and tell her mom to back the hell off. Your perspective might help her take a step back and realize her mom's actions aren't okay.

- On the other hand, if this has been going on for a while, your lady friend's self-worth might be pretty battered down, and a pep talk might not do the trick. Letting her know you're Worried that she's taking on way too much of her mom's poison and losing her mojo could snap her out of her funk. Backing this up with Openness about the fact that this has become a pattern could inspire the Courage she'll need to look at herself and why she's letting this go on.

Earth overcoming Water – There's a fabulous event going on at one of the local watering holes, and you and your bestie have hit the town in search of some hot, manly company. You're primed for your game, ready to dive on a grenade if need be, but your pal is sweaty and nervous, talking too fast and laughing that high pitched laugh of his – obviously, he's scared of striking out. Knowing that Fear is the negative expression of the Water Element, you can use Earth to overcome it.

- You can drag your buddy to a corner, grab him by the shoulders, and tell him Openly and honestly that he's got to pull it together. Get him to be Open to the fact that guys strike out sometimes, but they go home and they get over it. There are lots of studs in the bar, but you're not there to cure cancer, you're there to have a good time. If he can mirror your Openness to the facts – hell, you win some and you lose some – his Fear may dissipate.

- Since Fear and Anxiety are very close cousins, you could also mirror the way he's acting by dialing your own nervous habits up to eleven. See how he reacts – if you're being ridiculous enough, he should start looking at you like you're a total spaz. He may even ask you, "Dude, what the hell?" at which point you can drop the act and let him know he's been acting like that since you got there. Follow that up with the Openness described above, and he should hopefully find his game.

Some final tips about building with Earth:

- When you're figuring out how to start in any given situation, Earth is usually a safe bet. It's chill, not very flashy, and leaves lots of room for other people to contribute.

- While Openness is something you should always aspire to, don't be surprised if you feel confronted by it. It's almost reflexive for us to close ourselves off when things start getting real, so be prepared to have to work at it.

- The other thing about Openness is it goes both ways. You have to not only be honest about what's going on with you, but you have to be ready to accept what's going on with others and to not react with judgment.

- True Openness and grounding make it very difficult to throw you off your game. Staying down to Earth is your best defense against drama!

Metal – Taking a stand

It's hard not to see Metal as a pretty badass Element – they make guns with it, they make swords with it, they build cars out of it…the list goes on and on. As a race, we've valued Metal for thousands of years – we use common metals for tools, buildings, and transportation, and precious ones to show off how rich we are. The swordfighter's steel blade is a symbol not only of strength, but status as well.

Metal has three properties that tell us how it works energetically:

- Metal is strong and rigid, making it a powerful support
- Metal is heavy, making it challenging to wield
- Metal can be sharpened and used to penetrate other substances

Metal is associated with the color white, the positive emotions of Courage and Righteousness, and the negative emotion of Sorrow. These qualities share Metal's properties in several ways – Courage and Righteousness, when expressed fully, are both rigid like Metal; they're difficult to alter or change. Sorrow is certainly heavy, weighing down the soul, but Courage and Righteousness are like that too – you've got to be pretty strong to pick Courage up and wield it, and Righteousness is a heavy mantle to wear. All three emotions can cut through others, whether that's a positive or a negative thing.

Men who express lots of Metal tend to be pretty impressive. They seem to be in command, they're strong and confident, and they know how to get through life – the phrase "balls of steel" is perfect for these guys. An overload of Metal can turn a confident guy into a jackass real quick, though – anyone who goes past the tipping point with Righteousness is just begging to be taken down a peg. Also, being too rigid is never a good thing; it stunts growth (and makes people want to punch you). At the other end of the spectrum, a lack of Metal might make a man seem spineless, wimpy, whiny, and weak.

A great example of Metal in action can be seen in Eric Bana's portrayal of the hot and doomed elder Trojan prince Hector in the 2004 muscles-on-parade action-epic, Troy. Unlike the too-pretty-to-die prince Paris, Hector is Courageous and stoic in his convictions, even in the face of his impending death. We see the heavy Sorrow in his heart as he says goodbye to his wife and son, already knowing his fate. Still, he wears the mantle of Courage and Righteousness with dignity as he leaves Troy to meet Achilles on the battlefield, understanding that he won't survive.

So how can Metal be used?

When a guy busts out with Metal, he often undergoes a physical change – his posture becomes straighter, his voice becomes more commanding, and you can almost see the armor of Courage or Righteousness covering his body.

In the cycle of Elements, Metal creates Water and overcomes Wood. That means Courage or Righteousness (Metal) can create Gentleness (Water) or overcome Anger (Wood). Applying the negative emotions, Sorrow (Metal) can create Fear (Water) or overcome Kindness (Wood).

For example:

Metal creating Water – Your best friend is having a rough patch with his boyfriend. He's usually cool, but you can tell some of his insecurities have worked their way into the relationship, and now he's lashing out at everybody, especially his man. Wherever these issues are coming from, you know some Gentleness could nudge things in the right direction and possibly win the forgiveness of his sweetheart. Since Gentleness is an attribute of Water, you'll need Metal to help grow that.

- This situation calls for a bit of tact, and you can probably expect some resistance. Expressing Courage in this instance could just involve you acknowledging that this is none of your business, but it was important enough for you to step out of line and let him know he's screwing up. It takes balls to tell a friend to chill and treat his man better, but if he respects your opinion, he may be more willing to try the Gentle approach if you suggest it. Righteousness could work here too, especially if your buddy prides himself on treating men well – call him out on the fact that he's not living up to his own standards and he'll be forced to re-examine his behavior. This is especially true if he looks up to you.

- On the other hand, if this situation has really persisted and gotten bad, you can invoke Sorrow – let him know how sad it is that he's letting insecurity to get in the way of his relationship (you've got to be genuinely sad, though, or you're just laying a guilt trip). Nobody likes seeing a friend throw away something good, but too often we keep our mouths shut about it. Telling him the situation sucks and that he can do something about it by not trying to force everything might make a positive difference.

Metal overcoming Wood – Maybe here you're fighting with the boyfriend. He's all pissed off because you had to work extra hours and missed a big date he had planned. You've apologized, but he feels unappreciated and is letting you know it really, really loudly. Obviously, your man is Angry, which is governed by Wood. Being the alchemist you are, you know that Metal can overcome it.

- In this situation, invoking the Righteousness of Metal needs to be done from a very calm, Yin place, or you're going to come across like a pompous ass. Instead, remind both of you what you look like at your very best – by being the guy whose strength of character attracted him in the first place. Calmly and sincerely apologize for letting him down, explaining that you never would have done so without a good reason, and that the living you earn is part of the stability you like to offer in a relationship. After all, a man who shirks his responsibilities can't be relied on. Then ask him how you can make it up to him.

- Alternatively, letting him know how Sad and disappointed you are (sincerely letting him know, that is, don't invoke Sorrow unless you're really feeling it) that the evening didn't go as planned may help defuse his Anger. You don't want to be obnoxious or whiny about it, just express that you're bummed and that you're sorry. Then bring the Righteousness back in by letting him know you want to make it right and be the guy he can count on.

Some final tips for wielding Metal:

- When donning the mantle of Righteousness, be sure you're coming from a place that's right. Righteousness means being the guy who's true to himself, who others would admire, and whose conduct is correct. It doesn't mean pointing out the shortcomings in others.

- Metal is especially troublesome when it gets out of whack or when it's relied upon too much. Its rigidity can start to become a problem if it's there all the time – basically the balls of steel can become a steel rod up your ass (and not in a fun way). Nobody wants to be around someone like that. Instead of busting out with Metal right away, think of it more like a secret weapon you use only when necessary. When the job's done, put the piece away and go back to being flexible.

Water – Going with the flow

Water is arguably the most powerful of the Elements. While it lacks the badass qualities of Fire and Metal, in big enough quantities and with enough time, Water alone has the ability to destroy all four other Elements. Backed up by the force of gravity, Water is an Element to be reckoned with. The surfer who rides the waves and stays upright has learned to tap into its power by going with the flow. Plus, Water's one of the main ingredients in beer, which makes it even more fabulous.

Water has three properties that tell us how it works energetically:

- Water always seeks to level itself out
- Water finds even the smallest of openings and moves through them
- Water is highly adaptable – it can be raging or still; also solid, liquid, or vapor

Water is associated with the colors blue and black, the positive attribute of Gentleness and the negative emotion of Fear. Despite its immense power, the strength of Water is always expressed gently, slightly pushing and pushing until its obstacle gives in. Water doesn't force, it persists. Fear is like Water by being so damn pervasive – no matter how sure you are of yourself, small feelings of fear can seep through the cracks, eventually building into a flood.

Guys who exhibit lots of Water tend to be really chill – like Earth guys, they don't let much ruffle their feathers; they just adapt to the new circumstance. Water is a lot easier to demonstrate as you get older and figure out that obstacles can always be overcome, that the flow will always change direction sooner or later, and that there just aren't many things worth getting all bent out of shape over. Too much Water can make a guy seem endlessly wishy-washy, not willing to commit to any one course of action, or fearful to make waves. Too little can make him brittle and tactless, too forceful and insistent, dried up and stuck in his own way of thinking.

The best example I've seen of the power of Water is Yoda from the Star Wars series. Being a Jedi Master and all that, he's pretty wise, always keeping a level head, responding and adapting to his environment as needed. Basically all the major actions he takes are in response to what's happening around him, seeking to balance out the circumstances at hand (and, you know, the galaxy and shit). Even though he always waits for others to act before he responds, his self mastery ensures the amount of force (and Force) he brings to bear is pretty damn impressive.

So how can Water be used?

When a man invokes Water, he becomes focused, distant, adaptable, and cool. He's in control of the amount of force he's using, totally centered, flexible, and difficult to throw off course.

In the cycle of Elements, Water creates Wood and overcomes Fire. That means Gentleness (Water) can create Kindness (Wood) or overcome Hatred and Cruelty (Fire). Applying the negative emotions, Fear (Water) can create Anger (Wood) or overcome Love (Fire). As anyone who's ever been scared can testify, Fear is a very powerful motivator, though relying on it too much to get what you want can turn you into an insufferable asshole.

For example:

Water creating Wood – Let's say your man is pissed off at his best friend for some reason – apparently he said something out of line and really hurt your guy's feelings. You know the best friend has been under some stress lately, so it's possible he did act like a bitch, but you also know your boyfriend is taking it way too personally. Loath as you are to get involved in the drama, you don't want to see one comment get blown out of proportion and cause needless conflict. A little Kindness would probably make a huge difference here, and we need Water to create that.

- Your first option is to approach with Gentleness, sympathizing with your boyfriend and agreeing that his friend was out of line. Let him talk it out. After venting for long enough, eventually he'll run out of steam. From there, gently suggest that his friend's behavior was out of character, and that you both know he's under stress and probably sorry. If you can wear down the harshness of your guy's hurt feelings and get him to do something nice as a peace offering, the situation should resolve itself.

- If the tirade has gotten really bad and your man's Anger has gotten disproportionate to the situation, a scare tactic might be necessary to flip his switch and lead him to behave with some Kindness. Having already acknowledged that his friend was uncool, present him a worst-case scenario that will force him to reconsider his wounded pride – "What if he's sick/jobless/depressed/etc and that's why he's acting like this? Wouldn't you feel bad for making such a big deal out of it?" With any luck, your man will realize Kindness will get much more accomplished than petty Anger.

Water overcoming Fire – Let's say you work with an arrogant douche bag that thinks he can push everybody around and act like the Donald to get what he wants. He doesn't seem to get that nobody likes him, even if he did, it doesn't stop him from behaving like he owns the place. Recently, you two butted heads over an account he wanted to bend the rules on and you didn't let it happen. Now he's giving you shitty looks and sending barely-civil emails about work stuff – clearly, this guy Hates your guts. Instead of adding fuel to the Fire, you know you can use Water to put it out.

- In this instance, Gentleness is much more akin to the way you'd handle pressure-sensitive explosives than sitting in friendship circles and listening to each other's problems. You want to nudge – not force – the situation in the right direction. One option is to catch the guy doing something right and publicly acknowledge it. Send him and his boss an email praising how he handled a situation – he may reassess his Hatred of you if you make him look good for doing the right thing. At the very least, if he continues to be a jackass, it's clear you're not the one with a problem.

- Using Fear in this situation should only be a last resort, and only if the situation has really deteriorated. I actually dealt with this once – the guy came into my office and tried to intimidate me over a call with a client I'd followed up with – he thought I was undermining his account, but I was actually helping him out. He stepped into my personal bubble and spoke in a low tone, asking me if I thought he didn't know how to do his job. Coolly, calmly, I looked him square in the eye and stated my case. I didn't get emotional; I just stated the facts. I also didn't step back or apologize – my words were professional, but my subtext was loud and clear: I'm not afraid of you. My lack of Fear took the air out of his tires and his Fire went out quickly, defusing the situation.

Some final tips for navigating Water:

- Water is the most Yin of all the Elements, so invoking it requires you to first step back – wait – and then respond.
- Consciously responding with Water requires a calm heart and a level head. If you're emotionally charged, it's much harder to be Gentle than if you're detached. Clearing away your internal clutter makes it much more likely you'll handle the situation delicately.
- Using Water's ability to gently penetrate obstacles (hehe, yes, I said penetrate) requires patience above all else. It's much more like wearing down a wall with erosion than blasting through it with dynamite. It takes longer to do, sure, but sometimes it's counterproductive to leave rubble and shrapnel everywhere.
- You'll know when you've got a good handle on the Water Element when you adapt quickly to different emotional situations without

getting all wound up or sucked into the drama. When you can defuse interpersonal issues with the precision of a bomb expert, you know you've learned to surf the waves with skill.

Wood – Branching out

No guys, not that kind of wood.

Wood is the final Element in the cycle; our last stop before we come full circle with Fire. It's humble and common, but totally essential – we build our houses with it, burn it for fuel, and trees help make the oxygen we breathe. Wood helps us come together in a safe place, just like the carpenter who builds us places to live.

Wood has three properties that tell us how it works energetically:

- Wood grows from a small chute to a large tree, expanding over time
- Wood is both strong and flexible, acting as a support without being rigid
- Wood grows toward light, adapting to reach what nourishes it

Wood is associated with the color green, the positive attribute of Kindness, and the negative emotion of Anger. These qualities are like Wood in several ways – they both tend to start small and end up big, like a tiny gesture that is rewarded tenfold, or a little irritation that blows up into a full-scale fight. Both are common fallback emotions; all too often, people resort to Anger first, but their lack of rigidity makes them easier to influence. They also grow toward what feeds them – ever notice how people who are pissed off all the time congregate together?

Men who express lots of Wood tend to be gregarious, but less obviously so than Fire guys – instead of burning bright, they branch out, connecting with people one at a time. These are the guys who can draw anybody into a conversation, bending and wrapping around others' needs to become fast friends. They tend to be good at picking men up. Too much Wood can make a guy seem over-ingratiating and needy, clingy, and weird, and all that niceness can turn nasty if it's not returned. On the other hand, a lack of Wood makes a guy seem stale and stiff, inaccessible, and hard to get to know.

A lovely demonstration of Wood's power can be seen in Ken Watanabe's portrayal of the Chairman in the 2005 film adaptation of Memoirs of a Geisha. His Kindness toward the heroine fuels her entire story arc, starting as a small act of generosity that grows into a passionate, consuming Love on her part. He acts with consummate Kindness toward everyone around him, even to his own detriment, fueling much of the development of the other characters. Ultimately, the Love that grows from his Kindness is returned to him.

So how can Wood be used?

When a man invokes Wood, he can fit into most social situations – when we say that someone grows on us, it's because of Wood in action. Wood's combined sturdiness and flexibility totally rock when it comes to making attachments.

In the cycle of Elements, Wood creates Fire and overcomes Earth. That means Kindness (Wood) can create Love (Fire) or overcome Worry and Anxiety (Earth). Applying the negative emotions, Anger (Wood) can create Hatred or Cruelty (Fire) or overcome Openness (Earth). Much like Fear, Anger can certainly be used to motivate others, and in some cases, it's necessary – but don't rely on it too much, or you'll find yourself with lots of enemies.

For example:

Wood creating Fire: This one is classic. Let's say you've noticed your man has been a bit indifferent lately. Not necessarily cold or bitchy, but certainly not as affectionate as he used to be. You don't think there's another guy because he's not acting weird, but you'd like to see his eyes light up again when he looks at you. You know you want to stoke the

Fire, and Wood is just the element to do it.

- It's surprising how often the simple fact that Kindness generates Love gets overlooked. While simple gestures of Kindness can certainly make big differences – it's cliché, but flowers are a near-guaranteed pants-dropper when not overdone – the guy who knows his partner well can really make it count. Take it upon yourself to do something you know he'll appreciate. Wash his car if it's dirty. Do the laundry. Cook him a meal. Unless he's got his period, the Love should grow.

- If this situation has dragged on and Kindness hasn't done the trick, Anger might be needed to make him realize what his indifference is doing to your relationship. Let him know that you're willing to fight for what you have, but you won't be left waiting on the sidelines. Back this up with Kindness by showing you're there to give what it takes, and don't forget to be Kind to yourself – he's got to be as invested as you are, or it just isn't worth it.

Wood overcoming Earth: Let's say one of your buddies, who's a bit nervous on a good day, is having a full-fledged Anxiety freakout about something or other. He's a nice guy, really smart, but sometimes he lives in his head and lets his worries get the better of him. Since Worry and Anxiety are attributes of Earth, you know Wood can overcome it.

- Your first option is to distract your friend by doing something nice for him. It may be as simple as spending some time drinking beer, shooting the shit, and watching The Golden Girls to pull him out of the weird space he's in. If there's something he's wanted to do but has been too chicken, offer to go along – maybe he'll snap out of it. Sometimes Kindness means just being there.

- On the other hand, after dealing with this long enough, it's bound to wear a bit thin, and it's okay to get pissed about it. If your buddy's Anxiety is controlling his life, sharing your honest Anger about the situation may get him to realize he needs some help. If you can neutralize the Worry for long enough, maybe he'll take the steps he needs to take to fix it.

Some final tips for growing Wood:

- Trees take a while to grow – accordingly, so do relationships. The real value of Wood shows up over time, as acts of Kindness are carried out again and again. You'll see your measure in the eyes of others grow strong, deep roots.

- Being strong and flexible at the same time is something lots of guys struggle with – often they can do one or the other. Being flexible just means not being too stuck on your own version of the truth, being willing to bend, not being stubborn. Being strong means being willing to show Kindness in the face of adversity. Men who can do both at the same time are a cut above the rest.

- Beware how easily Anger can take root and make itself at home. Use it when it's useful, but beyond that, don't hang onto it. After Anger has done its job, cut it down. Life's too short to hold grudges.

Elements of Masculinity Conclusion from Sarina

Isn't that amazing? I think I read each of these twice. Just start playing with it and see what happens. Like any new technology, you will need to practice. Maybe keep the book in your pocket for reference? We'd love it if you experimented and let us know how you did.

Again, remember what Obi Wan said in Star Wars and use your power for good. If you misuse your power, we can't be held responsible for what happens next.

Good luck guys.

Now, on to the next chapter…

CHAPTER 5
Personality Types

Here are just a few of the personality types you may run into when dealing with gay men. Forewarned is forearmed.

If you have read any of the other books in the Tequila series, you know that there is always a story or ten peppered through these Types.

Enjoy,

Sarina

The Marlboro Man

The Marlboro Man is a figure used in tobacco advertising campaign for Marlboro cigarettes. In the United States, where the campaign originated, it was used from 1954 to 1999. The Marlboro Man was first conceived by Leo Burnett in 1954. The image involves a rugged cowboy or cowboys, in nature with only a cigarette. The advertisements were originally conceived as a way to popularize filtered cigarettes, which at the time were considered feminine.

The Marlboro advertising campaign, created by Leo Burnett Worldwide, is said to be one of the most brilliant advertisement campaigns of all time. It transformed a feminine campaign, with the slogan "Mild as May", into one that was masculine in a matter of months. Although there were many Marlboro Men, the cowboy proved to be the most popular. This led to the "Marlboro Cowboy" and "Marlboro Country" campaigns.

"Every man I meet wants to protect me. I can't figure out what from."
-Mae West

Picture this scenario:

You meet this gorgeous man at a party. He is standing off to the side, watching the players with a gentle smile. You can just tell by looking at him, if chaos were to ensue, he'd have no problem taking care of himself and those around him (go wild with fantasies here). His attire is classic expensive casual wear that fits perfectly. He has mastered the art of looking like he's not trying. It's the Marlboro Man minus the stinky tobacco, yellowed teeth and prematurely aging skin. Miracle of miracles, he lets you know he's interested (without throwing himself at you, of course). JOY!

You have a few drinks, talk for a while, and he asks you if you'd like to go somewhere more private. This man is smart, cool, elegant, masculine and 100% sexy. The two of you go back to your place and have mind-bending sex for hours. He is so cool that he gets up afterwards and starts to get dressed without being asked. No weirdness, no odd comments, nothing to indicate an iota of insecurity or angst. *Of course*, any man this intriguing should be in your little black book, so you have to ask for his number. He doesn't ask for yours, gives you his, and leaves with a smile.

Here's what you need to know:

A true Marlboro Man personality type is exactly what he portrayed when you met him; cool elegance with a rugged sense of earthiness and raw yet private sensuality. He is the opposite of a Drama Queen. This does not mean he is unfeeling or cold, his expression of emotion is subdued and often more thought out. There is no "norm" for how they react to passionate men, by the way, so be yourself and let the chips fall where they may if you are dating one.

That being said, buyer beware. If you've been around the block at all, you should have figured out by now that frequently men are not what they appear to be at first glance. The Marlboro Man can be an act, or a very small piece of a far more complex personality. It is nearly impossible to tell if this is a true Marlboro Man unless you get to know him; and therein lies the rub.

Three months later you might discover that underneath the detached exterior is a vulnerable person who is far more interested in commitment than he led on. Marlboro Men tend to have a coat of armor that covers a sensitive core.

There are a number of reasons men become the Marlboro Man; here are a few:

1. Intimacy makes him uncomfortable. That's not necessarily a deal breaker; most of us have that issue to some degree at some point in our lives.
2. He has no interest getting to know you and is being aloof or polite in your presence.
3. He really is that comfortable with himself.

Unlike some other Personality Types, the Marlboro Man isn't necessarily a problem Personality. He may be a genuinely decent person. He may also be a closet scary guy, so be careful not to judge this book by its cover.

Can I date a Marlboro Man?

Maybe. Why not get to know him and then you could just ask?

Look, a true Marlboro Man may or may not want to get close to you. They all have different agendas. What makes them cool is that they won't push you to be or feel something that isn't there. What makes them un-cool to some is that they tend not to be flowery or overly affectionate, especially in public. A true Marlboro Man is for you independent, low-maintenance fellows who appreciate subtlety and low drama.

Why Real Men Drink Straight Tequila – Part 1

Hosting a radio show can be fun. Here's a great example.

"Hey lover, welcome to Couple Chat, tell me your tale." is a pretty normal way for me to open a show.

The man on the other line was almost giddy as he launched right in and described the stranger he'd met the night before.

"He was understated elegance in leather boots and jeans."

The caller was pretty proud of himself for lassoing this classy man into coming over for a nightcap at two in the morning. The long and the short of it was that the usual ensued and they were naked in no time. They hung from the rafters, and swung from the chandelier – as I said, the usual.

What was not usual for our caller was when the fireworks were over and it was time to sleep, the elegant stranger got up, got dressed, and left with a warm smile and a twinkle in his eye. He did not pretend he would be back. As a matter of fact, the caller had to ask for a phone number (yes, it was real; he checked).

"So, what can I do for you? It sounds like you just had every man's wet dream last night."

"Yeah, I thought so too, Sarina," said the caller, "but now I don't know what to do. I mean, does he want me to call? I want to see him again, I think. I don't know. What do you think?"

I explained that the first step was to make up his mind. Then the line dedicated to Eric Thurnbeck, my fellow Tao counselor, lit up.

"Hey Eric! Welcome to Couple Chat, old friend. What's on your mind?"

"Pardon me for stating the obvious, but I think your caller only has one course of action here." chirped Eric live over the airwaves. "Dude, if you want to know what this elegant stranger wants from you, *call him and ask.* If he's really cool, he'll tell you what he wants in clear concise terms." Eric paused, and then added, "The question is, can you handle his answer?"

I had absolutely nothing to add to that and neither did anyone else.

The Manchild

man |man|[1]

noun (pl. **men** |men|)

1. an adult human male.

-   a husband, boyfriend, or lover: *the two of them lived for a time as man and wife.*
-   [with adj.] a male person associated with a particular place, activity, or occupation: *a Harvard man | I'm a solid union man.*
-   a male pursued or sought by another, esp. in connection with a crime: *Inspector Bull was sure they would find their man.*
-   dated: a manservant or valet: *get me a cocktail, my man.*
-   historical: *a vassal.*

2. a human being of either sex; a person: *God cares for all races and all men.*

-   (also **Man**) [in sing.] human beings in general; the human race: *places untouched by the ravages of man.*
-   [in sing.] an individual; one: *a man could buy a lot with eighteen million dollars.*
-   a person with the qualities often associated with males such as bravery, spirit, or toughness: *she was more of a man than any of them.*
-   [in sing.] a type of prehistoric human named after the place where the remains were found: *Cro-Magnon man.*

child |CHīld|

noun (pl. children |'CHildrən|)

a young human being below the age of puberty or below the legal age of majority.

-   a son or daughter of any age.
-   an immature or irresponsible person: *she's such a child!*

- a person who has little or no experience in a particular area: he's a child in financial matters.

"For many, immaturity is an ideal, not a defect." -Mason Cooley

Here's the scenario:

You're at the bar and meet this wacky, beautiful boy. He dresses a little funky, laughs a lot, and isn't afraid to look you in the eye and smile right away. You buy him drinks. You take him for coffee at midnight and end up going back to your place. In the morning, he comes out of the bathroom wearing nothing but one of your button up work shirts and looks amazing in it. The two of you christen the kitchen counter, table, and floor. He does not care that you are late for work and neither do you (until you get there and your boss is fuming).

This boy is completely carefree and whimsical.

After he leaves, you realize he left behind his incredibly sexy boxer shorts (with little skulls and crossbones), so you call his mobile to tell him. Hmm, wrong number. Weird. Well, you gave him your number, so you're sure he'll call.

He does not.

However, ten days later there's a knock on your door at about 1:30 in the morning; there he is in all his boyish splendor. He's even sexier than you remember. He throws himself in to your arms and before you know it, you're doing the nasty.

In the morning, before he leaves, but after you've christened the sofa, you ask him for his mobile number again. He changes the subject by proving you actually *can* sustain an erection right after you have sex. Not sure how he did that, but he did. You have to leave for work and he lets you know that he forgot his wallet so he'll be walking downtown. You, of course, give the boy a ride and then give him $30. I mean, he'd do the same for you, right?

Three months later, you've christened the entire house, the back yard, and the alley. You never know when he'll come around, but when he does, you have an amazing sexual adventure. He's never treated for dinner or even cocktails and you still don't actually have his number or know where he lives, but no one else compares to this wild crazy Manchild.

HERE'S WHAT YOU DON'T KNOW:

A) He lives with his mother.

B) You are not the only one.

C) He seems unreal because he is.

D) He does not have a job (even if he told you he does).

Who dates a The Man-child personality type?

We don't actually *date* these boys. We spend time with them, have sex with them, skip work, try new things, and treat when we go out because they seem to have no wallets, but "dating" would be a bit of a stretch being that you know almost nothing about him.

Man-child personality types are perfect for you if you are looking for a fun way to avoid intimacy. Like children, these boys are playing a game. On some level, each of us has a sense of who we are dealing with. Those who willingly become involved with Manchild personality types are making the choice to stay in a relationship that has no chance of maturing. They stand firm in a relationship whose only boundary is… depth. If this is you, then you are going to have some entertaining experiences with an intimate stranger. If it's ok that he is uninterested in growing closer to you (or growing at all), then you're doing great. You will know his name (maybe) and various other necessary details, but that's about it. There is a place for that, however even the kinkiest of guys knows that after the party is over, it is wise to spend a few minutes connecting to your lover and making sure everyone is ok before parting. I mean, you may actually see each other again or make a friend if a genuine connection is made, even if that connection is just sex.

You can't blame the Manchild personality type for throwing the party when you signed him on to have it in the first place. Remember, he's just doing what you knew he would do – there's no mystery here, no duping – and any lies that you might have fallen for are only painted scenery on the villa you've been willingly renting by dating him in the first place. There are no victims here either, and there certainly should be no surprises.

So let me repeat; if you can't blame the Manchild for a relationship that is all fluff and no substance, then *who started* this party?

That's right; it's you…again.

Let's go deeper

You want to know why we can't keep seeing Manchild personality types for a prolonged period of time? It's because it takes too much energy (life force – Chi). It takes energy to maintain that willing suspension of disbelief. It takes energy to pretend that we're okay with wading hip-deep in bullshit … even if it's our own.

We all want a little romance in our lives, but there comes a time when the burping, and scratching, and (heavens forbid) farting – not to mention the bill paying – become necessary evils in *every* evolving relationship. If you become involved with a Manchild, don't expect him to grow up. You are also missing the opportunity for a mutually responsible relationship that breaks beyond the surface. That spot of heaven where the relationship is more teamwork than tryst is where you discover that though the person you are with may not be your fantasy, he certainly is a dream come true.

There is a time and place for everything, so if you need to take a vacation, feel free to take a Manchild personality type with you. He will make your holiday a memorable one. But remember, when the vacation is over, leave your Manchild in the fairy tale book (or porn magazine) where he belongs.

Why Real Men Drink Straight Tequila – Part 2

"I can't cum anymore."

"That's not ok." I answered. "When did it start?"

"A few weeks ago. It just sort of stopped. I was with one of my sweeties, a guy I've known for almost a year, and I just couldn't get into it. Then, it happened again with a man I usually have amazing sex with. No matter who I'm with, or where we are, I just can't ..."

The man on the phone trailed off and left our listening audience hanging. About 150,000 people were waiting for a brilliant, sexy answer from yours truly.

"Let me get this straight" I said. "You've got two lovers?"

"Uh, not exactly. I have six at the moment." The anonymous man was surprisingly coy as he spoke now.

"Six? Wow. Ok. So, monogamy clearly hasn't been your thing. Question: do any of these men love you?"

"Four of them say they do. One of them can't even sleep when I'm at his house because he's paranoid I'll leave."

"Do you have a habit of leaving in the night? I asked

"Oh, I've done that one or two *hundred* times."

"When was the last time you lavished one of your lovers with flowers and chocolate for no reason?"

"I don't need to do that. Besides, I don't even have a job."

"Ok, got it. You don't have a job, but get by because you have sex in exchange for free stuff. Aren't you clever?" I said. "Do you have feelings for any of these men?"

"Sure, they're all my favorite – when I'm with them." Now he was chuckling.

"I see. Last question; when was the last time you brought one of them back to your place?"

"Never. Mom wouldn't approve. She's a good Catholic gal."

"Right. Is there anything else I should know?"

"Not really. I just want my mojo back. This sucks. Can I say suck on the air?"

"Sure, if you are referring to removing snake venom." I took a deep breath and continued. "I hope you are open to change, because that's what's happening. A lot of people engage in casual sex, some with multiple partners. You know it's your thing if it gives you and your lovers pleasure. But guess what? You just stopped receiving pleasure. You, Tao brother, are done. Now you have to ask yourself, 'What's next?' if you want to activate your sweet spot again."

"I don't get it." The guy moaned.

"Sure you do. That's why you're whining. You've been this elusive, crazy, sexy, wild mystery to men all over town. It used to be erotic. It used to be profitable. Now, it's just boring and immature. Leave the game behind and dive a little deeper. If you listen to your body, it will tell you what it needs to be healthy and happy. This isn't it any more. Again, it's time for a change."

Silence.

"Ever thought about falling in love? I mean, that might involve being real, sharing your feelings and growing up, are you up for that?"

The man on the line was still silent. My personal favorite when we're recording live.

"Hello. Are you still there?" I asked. Apparently not, the line was dead. Our mystery man had vanished, once again before the climax.

The Nester

nester[2]

noun

1 [usu. with adj.] a bird that nests in a specified manner or place.

"Would you like me to seduce you?" Mrs. Robinson – *The Graduate*

Nesters are men whose main focus is to create a home with another person. Who that person is tends to be damned near irrelevant in the choosing process.

Your classic Nesters are extremely comfortable in your home right away - and rightly so, they are about to move in. He conveniently "forgets" his toothbrush in your bathroom after the second time he sleeps over (why the hell did he bring a toothbrush anyway?). You can nudge him in the morning and say, "Hey, I have to go to work." and he will groggily respond "OK honey, see you when you get home." He's probably referring to you as his "boyfriend" right now as he talks on the phone while lying in your bed.

Shocking, but it happens every day.

Now, if you've got a strong spine, you will invite them to get the hell up and get the hell out when you leave. You may even feel a trickle of perspiration roll down your face as you lock that door behind the both of you.

But, if you are weak and just can't bear to hurt his feelings, you may have a five-course meal waiting for you after work. Your plants will be watered, your laundry clean, dry, and folded.

While some men want to invade your mind and home simply because they are serial Lonely Guys or just men who don't like living alone, other Nesters who initiate cohabitating right away often just need a place to sleep or someone to share bills with. This is a classic separation in perspective and should be considered.

Who the hell would date a Nester more than once or twice?

Nesters should partner with other Nesters!

Why not? If both people are into living together and sharing their lives, it could work. Both of you should want a live-in lover and a companion at home. You will figure out if this was an intelligent move later. This is The Nester way.

Why Real Men Drink Straight Tequila – Part 3

My boyfriend, Gary Parker, frequently comes to the radio station when we record the show. I try to prevent him from causing trouble, but you know how you guys are. He actually owns the station, and my contract, and on occasion does something that makes me want to kill him just a little.

So, I'm talking to this man, live on the air, and he's freaking out because his "boyfriend" doesn't want him to move in after six weeks of dating. He is inconsolable and I am showing compassion even though it is clear that he is asking for something his man does not want to give.

"Why? We care for each other. We sleep over at each other's houses all the time. Why can't we live together? What's his problem?"

Before I even had a chance to answer, a loud voice came over the air and broke our conversation.

"Tell this lunatic to get his crap out of that man's house, stop bugging him, get naked, and shut the heck up." Followed by roaring laughter from the folks in the control room.

You'd think after years in the business Gary would know the difference between the little button which allows him to speak in to my headset and the button that connects him, live, to the actual call.

Thanks, honey.

The Kinkster

kinky | kiNGkē| adjective

1 involving or given to unusual sexual behavior.

2 having kinks or twists:

kinkily |-kilē | adverb ,

kinkiness noun

"In the end, you will submit…It's got to hurt a little bit." – New Order, *Sub-Culture*

Most of us know, are, or were this guy. The Kinkster personality types are those guys whose masculine and romantic identity is largely defined by their inquisitive and explorative sexuality. This isn't necessarily a bad thing if they are *also* identified by their intellect, wit, honesty, and charm.

If you have been a gay man for more than five minutes, you have already seen the scenario below:

John is a conservative real estate broker in DC. He meets Tom at happy hour and the two become lovers. Tom's amazing repertoire of sexual tastes blows John away and for the first few months the newness of it all is intoxicating. A little B&D with a side order of role playing and everyone is elated. John is trying new things and Tom is an excellent teacher who creates a safe space for experimentation.

A year later when Tom would like to invite others in to the role playing and the B&D is leaving scars, John is feeling turned off and sex is becoming less frequent and less acceptable.

Two years later, John and Tom are still a couple; however, the relationship has more of an "open" twist. John has returned to a state of conservatism and prefers traditional vanilla-type sex while other lovers have been brought to Tom's bed to satisfy his sexual needs. John tries to understand and Tom tries not to feel vilified, deviant or rejected.

Who dates the Kinkster successfully?

For starters other Kinksters! Hello! Doesn't it just make sense? Some men grow out of the exploration phase and some keep the hotness sizzling. Men in their 70's and 80's remain sexually active while some step out of the game in their 50's.

This is not to say that sex should be the only foundation for a lasting relationship, but it also stands to reason that if a man intends to cultivate a lasting relationship he should examine sexual compatibility as one of the components. Therefore, Kinksters UNITE!

It comes down to compatibility, ground rules and love. If basic sexual compatibility exists from the onset of the relationship, ground rules feel less confining and the expression of love and playfulness occurs naturally.

Why Real Men Drink Straight Tequila – Part 4

The clock on the wall said 9:25am; time for a musical interlude. We always play some slinky blues and headline news during the breaks. It is, after all, a radio show.

Gary and I went downstairs to the coffee room. I knew exactly how to use nine out of the eleven minutes (get your mind out of the gutter). I keep some yummy homemade Chai in the fridge that I am convinced keeps my boyfriend in love with me.

Granted, we were talking pretty loud; it wasn't enough to break sound barriers or glass when we walked in to the tiny room.

"Hey," he groaned, "lower the volume a notch."

A sickly man in his mid-thirties was sitting alone, head in hands, elbows propped on the table. He was naturally handsome, but not today. Today, he was actually sort of greenish and we just stared for a few seconds because he was clearly wearing clothes from the night before. Darrell was a permanent figure around the station and everyone loved him. On a regular day, he had flaming red hair and ivory skin. He had been the head janitor for eight years, longer than I had my show by a long shot.

"Darrell, what the hell happened?" Gary asked sympathetically. "Are you OK?"

"Ohhhh, it's all coming back to me now." He shook his head. "Ohhhh, I'm never drinking tequila again."

"What happened, sweetheart?" I asked in a low, quiet voice so as not to exacerbate his obvious headache.

"It's sort of a blur. I screwed up real good this time." Again he groaned and held his head in his hands.

"Everything was just fine," he continued in his thick Midwest, small town accent, "until someone started buying shots. Then, it all went crazy.

See, there was this guy at the bar last night, and he was real sweet on me. I was partying with some of the boys from the newsroom and this guy ended up sittin' at our table. Heck, I think he was the one who bought the first round. Anyhow, I remember he was gettin' sorta touchy-feely under the table. I was all about it at first. But, after a while, he was gettin' kinda aggressive and the boys were getting protective; especially Johnny. I've never seen him so animated. It was actually pretty funny." He smiled and sort of went blank for a second as he stared into space.

"Johnny from accounting?" asked Gary.

"Yeah." he sort of mumbled.

I looked questioningly at Gary, and he said, "The short little bald dude who always brings home baked cookies to the Christmas Party."

"Ahh, got it."

"I remember telling Johnny and the guys to back off." Darrell continued. "I mean, yeah, the stranger was getting kinda forceful, but I hadn't written him off yet."

Silence.

"Then, I don't know exactly what happened. More shots, that much I know. Then there were handcuffs. And a blindfold. I got spanked for the first time since I was ten years old. You wouldn't believe the stuff he was into."

"Oh honey," I said filling two cups with chilled Chai, "We've all gone to bed with someone crazy." I could feel Gary boring holes in to the side of my skull with his gaze. I ignored it. "If you were sober, you would have realized that man wasn't right for you. You just took a walk on the wild side for one night, no big deal. It doesn't sound like you were really hurt, and besides, it's not like you ever have to see him again."

"Please stop." he said while shaking his head just a little. "I didn't wake up in the stranger's bed; that I could handle."

"You mean…" Gary said.

"Uh-huh." said Darrell staring blankly ahead again. "That short little bald dude rocked – my –world."

The Caretaker

caretaker |ˈke(ə)r,tākər|[3]

noun

1 a person employed to look after a public building or a house in the owner's absence.

- [as modifier] holding power temporarily: *his was a caretaker regime.*

2 a person employed to look after people or animals.

DERIVATIVES

caretake verb

"If you ever become a mother, can I have one of the puppies?"

-Charles Pierce

Have you ever hung out with a couple and had to sit there while one of them does something, in public, like lick his thumb and fix his partner's hair? Ever had a bro whose awesome bachelor pad became neat as a pin and started smelling good after he started dating a new guy? Have you, yourself, ever allowed a man to cook you a hideous meal for your health?

These are all things that happen in the presence of The Caretaker. To simplify, The Caretaker personality type wants to take care of you. This can be great if you want someone to do that. If you don't, he will make you nuts.

The Tao teaches us that balance is the key to peaceful outcomes. Here we employ the concept by becoming aware of The Caretaker's motive: Is he a conscious individual with time and love to spare or is he avoiding his own life by managing yours?

No one wants his lover to stop mid whipping-cream-coitus to check if he is lactose intolerant. No one wants to be reminded, "One more drink may impair your driving." For sure, no man wants some guy passing judgment on his living, eating, or spending.

---

3   New Oxford American Dictionary

Or, do they?

How do I know if my Caretaker boyfriend is coming from a balanced place?

If the action taken by your partner feels like a gift and adds value to your experience, it's probably coming from a balanced place. If your sweetie asks things of you he does not have in place for himself, look closer as he may be trying to live through you instead of participating in his own experience. If there are no strings attached to the giving, taking may be appropriate.

Lastly, if you are allowed to give back to this man even more than he gives to you, you may want to examine The Caretaker in yourself and see if you like him.

Who Dates The Caretaker personality type?

There are a few kinds of men who date The Caretaker type.

As I stated earlier, some guys actually want someone to do things for them. This has been happening for thousands of years. Eve said to Adam, "Hey! If you grab that apple, I'll let you fix my car." (A very little known biblical detail.) During the cave man era, men hunted, gathered and were eaten alive while their partners prepared yummy dishes in the cave, like Pterodactyl Eggs Florentine and Brontosaurus Burgers. In the Dark Ages, fops embroidered fancy scarves for their beloved knights before they went off to battle against perilous odds. Yes, there have been those lovelies who improve our lives by doing sweet little things since the dawn of time.

In the end, only you can determine if The Caretaker in question is a gift or a curse (whether it be your lover or yourself).

Why Real Men Drink Straight Tequila – Part 5

About three months ago I got a call-in…

"I am losing my mind!" cried the man live, on-air. "You know I've been seeing this man for a few months. I swear to God, this morning he had my clothes set out for me and actually expected me to wear them. What am I, five years old?"

Sam is a regular. He dates a lot. Let me reiterate, Sam dates a *lot*. His usual pattern is to start out madly in love and eventually lose interest because of something silly. He dumped a guy because he farted in his sleep; once. Anyone who listens to the show knows that Sam's stories always start and end the same. It's actually gotten sort of boring.

Fast-forward a few weeks. Sam lets us know that he is taking the pick-my-outfit guy on a tropical vacation. Hmm, interesting. I wonder if he'll iron his bathing suit?

Fast forward again to present day. "Hi Sam. What's the latest, old friend?"

"I'm getting married."

"What? I swear it sounded like you just said you're getting married."

"I finally get it," he said. "I read one of your books and really paid attention to The Caretaker Personality Type. And you know what? I want someone to do nice things for me. Is that so wrong?"

"Of course not, Sam. Uh, er, have you heard him fart yet?"

"Yep. You would have been proud of me; I still think he's really hot."

"Bravo! And how did this man tame our famous playboy?"

"Honestly, it sort of crept up on me. There were a few incidences where I got angry with him for cleaning my apartment, or leaving food in my fridge. Every time I would confront him, more like attack him actually, he would start crying and apologize. He has always said that he just likes doing nice things for me. Like that first time he set my clothes

Ch 5 Personality Types

out for work, I railed on him really bad for thinking I can't choose my own outfit. He had a total meltdown. He wanted to pamper me like I pamper him. I felt like a real dog making him cry like that.

Now, I feel totally different about the sweet things he does for me. I feel loved and supported."

"How new-age of you, Sam. Wait a second. Only a few months ago you felt invaded and disconnected. Did he change or something?"

"Sarina, I know a set up when I hear one. So, I'll save you the effort and confess that changing my perspective changed everything. Changing what I have it mean when he does something has changed my life. I see now that one point of view is that he is a dreaded Control Freak. Another point of view is that he is the kind of person who expresses appreciation and affection through being of service.

…and yes, I rehearsed that before I called."

"Sam?"

"Yes?"

"Congratulations. I think we're done here. I have just got my wish and become obsolete."

The Older Man

old[4]

adjective

1 having lived for a long time; no longer young: *the old man lay propped up on cushions.*

- made or built long ago: *the old quarter of the town.*
- possessed or used for a long time: *he gave his old clothes away.*
- having the characteristics or showing the signs of age: *marble now so old that it has turned gray and chipped.*

2 **the old days** a period in the past, often seen as significantly different from the present, esp. noticeably better or worse : *it was easier in the old days | we are less confident than in* **the good old days** | **the bad old days** *of incoherence and irresponsibility.*

old enough to be someone's father (or **mother**) informal of a much greater age than someone (esp. used to suggest that a romantic or sexual relationship between the people concerned is inappropriate).

"A woman over 40 will never wake you in the middle of the night to ask, 'What you are thinking?' She does not care what you think."

(Many people have received an email stating that this was a quote from Andy Rooney, the famous American commentator. In Fact, a columnist named Frank Kaiser wrote a version of this that was later embellished and attributed to Rooney.)

NOTE:

When we speak of the Younger Man, we refer to a man who is at least eight or ten years younger than you are now. In this context, older is a man 40 or older. He can be older than you or younger, just needs to be at least 40. Men over 40 are dramatically different than younger men, so it is worth writing about.

---

4   New Oxford American Dictionary

You go to a party at a friend's house one summer night. By the time you get there, everyone has been drinking for a while. There are the typical party types mingling with each other. Chatting by the bar-b-q are the couples. Single men and horny boys surround the bar. Holding court in the kitchen is some loud mouth guy, lying his ass off, and sucking in anyone who buys his bullshit. Drunk-boy is making out with a friend of yours on the sofa. You know, the usual.

"Excuse me, but do you know where the kitchen is?" You turn around to find an incredible man standing behind you. "I brought this Riesling and wanted to chill it for a while."

He's fit and pretty, but that's not what gets you. He's got a genuine smile and is looking you in the eyes. He is sexy in jeans and a button-down – his shoes are expensive and understated. There's an air of confidence about him that isn't stuck up. He's got a few laugh lines and on him they are *totally hot*. He smells amazing.

"Yeah," you brilliantly reply. "Follow me."

Once in the kitchen, the blowhard is still putting on a show. While searching for a spot for his wine in the fridge, the hot guy avoids the gaze of mister blowhard.

"Looking for something?" says blowhard while walking over to him, ignoring the men who were interested in his tale.

Hot guy straightens up, looks blowhard up and down, smiles and says, "There is nothing I want here, thank you."

Now, not all older men look like Sean Connery, and not all of them are stable human beings, but your chances of finding a self-confident, self-sufficient man who knows what he wants and doesn't bug you with insecurities dramatically increases after 40. The Older Man tends to be more dignified.

Unless he is an emotional mess, in which case, he goes to the kitchen, gets completely suckered by that cock-blocking dipstick holding court, and ends up in the bathroom with him in about five minutes. He knows what he wants and how to get it, even if he wants something crappy.

Actually, this still makes the Older Man pretty cool, doesn't it?

The Older Man has advantages and liabilities, just like the Younger

Man. When an Older Man grows up to be dysfunctional, he is a blown-up version of his younger counterpart. He can be stubborn and stuck in his ways or mature enough to let you make your own mistakes without trying to fix you.

The bottom line is that men become larger versions of themselves as they age. If he's cool at the core, he becomes very cool as the mystery of life fades and reality sets in. If his reality sucks, he will become that darkness and may pull out of it, but hasn't to this point, so be wary of starting a new relationship with a scary Older Man; he may not change as easily as a Younger Man.

Who would date the Older Man?

Any guy who does not want to play big daddy or be the hero will get along with the Older Man. If you are more interested in being individuals than "growing together", he's your guy. If you're OK sleeping next to a psychic, you may not mind that he sees right through your lame excuses and stories of victimization. Basically, the Older Man is only for the guy who has nothing to hide, doesn't need to be needed, and thinks self-confidence is sexy.

Don't fret if this isn't for you, this guy definitely is not for everyone. But, for the no-nonsense dude, the Older Man can be pretty sweet.

Why Real Men Drink Straight Tequila – Part 6

"Oh man, I got it bad.

I'm at the grocery store picking up the essentials: beer, frozen pizza, wine, milk, and spritzers. I turn the corner with my grocery cart and smash in to a very hot guy. You know, pretty eyes, tight sweater, understated boots and his ass is a-m-a-z-i-n-g. This guy really took care of himself.

Instead of getting angry because I rammed his cart, he starts laughing. Some green thing, I think was a vegetable, flew out and landed perfectly in my basket. Within minutes we're yucking it up and having a great time. I knew he was older, but I couldn't tell how much. He's got that playful sexy thing going along with an openness that sort of made me want to share my life story with him."

"Sounds sexy. What do you need from me?" I asked. "Or, do you have a question for our listeners?"

"Well that was six weeks ago," said the dude live on the air. "I've been dating him ever since. Let me start by saying he's the best lover I've ever had. I mean, I had no idea..." The man on the other line trailed off then started again. "Long story short, he's twelve years older than I am and there's some, uh, issues."

"Issues? Like what? By the way, how old are you?"

"I'm thirty two, he's..."

"Forty four." I interrupted.

"Yeah, forty four, but he looks better than a lot of men my age, Sarina. He's tight!"

"Ok, back to my original question, what do you need?"

"Well, I just feel like I'll never catch up to him. He makes more money than I do, he has more cool friends, he knows what he wants and how to get it. I'm just figuring things out, and I feel like a child around him sometimes."

"Hey, what's your name?" I asked.

"Larry, I'm from Wisconsin."

At that point Eric's line lit up, so I asked Larry from Wisconsin to hold on.

"Hey fabulous! What's shakin?"

"I have to ask the dude on the phone a question." he said. "Larry? You there?"

"Yeah! Hey, I loved your book."

"Our book." I corrected Larry.

Eric laughed right in to the phone for a few seconds, and then got serious. "Larry, does this man ever mention your shortcomings? I mean, does he say things that are emasculating or try to humiliate you?"

"No, he's actually pretty cool. When we go out, he always says he's had a good week at work and he wants to treat us to something nice. It's weird."

"Weird? I date older people too, dude. I like mature men when it comes to romantic intimacy." Eric got quiet for a moment. "Look, one of the things that I've learned from hanging out with older people is that we, as younger men, also bring something worthwhile to the relationship. It's different for everyone, but trust me, if you're treating him well, are up for some fun, open minded, and appreciate what he brings to the relationship that's worth a lot. What we add to a friendship with any person is who we are *inside*. You're old enough to pay your own bills and make your own decisions – trust me, he knows that. He's lucky to have you for all the reasons you don't even think about, like being honest or noticing how good his hair smells. You're lucky to have each other, actually."

I was completely swept up by the poetry of it all. That was beautiful and so true.

"Wow." said Larry. "I never thought about it that way."

"And besides," continued Eric, "older men know their bodies, aren't afraid to slow down and get to know yours, tend to have better self-control and more tricks up their, uh, sleeves. Better take your vitamins and get a grip on yourself – literally."

One brief shining moment of poetry, and they remembered they were dudes again.

The Impossible to Please

impossible |im'päsəbəl|[5]

adjective

not able to occur, exist, or be done: *a seemingly impossible task* | [with infinitive] : *it was almost impossible to keep up with him.*

- very difficult to deal with: *she was in an impossible situation.*
- informal (of a person) very unreasonable: *"Impossible woman!" the doctor complained.*

ORIGIN Middle English: from Old French, or from Latin **impossibilis**, from in- 'not' + possibilis

*please |plēz|

verb [with obj.]

1 cause to feel happy and satisfied: *he arranged a fishing trip to please his son* | [with obj. and infinitive] : ***it pleased*** *him to be seen with someone in the news.*

- [no obj.] give satisfaction: *she was quiet and eager to please.*
- satisfy aesthetically.

2 (**please oneself**) take only one's own wishes into consideration in deciding how to act or proceed: *this is the first time in ages that I can just please myself.*

- [no obj.] wish or desire to do something: *feel free to wander around* ***as you please****.*
- (it pleases, pleased, etc., someone to do something) dated it is someone's choice to do something: *instead of attending the meeting, it pleased him to go off hunting.*

adverb

used in polite requests or questions: *please address letters to the Editor* | *what type of fish is this, please?*

- used to add urgency and emotion to a request: please, please come home!

---

5   New Oxford American Dictionary

- used to agree politely to a request: *"May I call you at home?"* *"Please do."*

- used in polite or emphatic acceptance of an offer: *"Would you like a drink?"* *"Yes, please."*

- used to ask someone to stop doing something of which the speaker disapproves: *Rita, please—people are looking.*

- used to express incredulity or irritation: *You cleaned out the barn in only two hours? Oh, please!*

"Into the garbage chute, flyboy." – Princess Leia, Star Wars

Spotlight on the beautiful boy dancing alone at the club. He is an Adonis. He is confident. He is surrounded by men and couldn't care less. If you are suave enough to grab his attention, he looks you up and down, and then acts like you are invisible. In a brave "liquid courage" moment, you send the boy a house Jell-O Shot and the waiter returns to let you know that the gentleman only drinks champagne cocktails – Dom Perignon preferred.

You have just encountered The Impossible to Please zone.

Now, make no mistake, this guy could be short, tall, thin, fat, rich or poor; it's up to you. The Impossible to Please is the guy you wish you could have, but never get because *he is a stuck up princess who withholds his approval, often milking his victims of money and self-esteem in the process.*

His name is always Troy.

We chase that which retreats, so the challenge of a diva who cannot be pleased registers as something to be chased if we are not careful. It probably goes back to the cave man days when our ancestors had to compete to catch the best food, lodging and sexual conquests. If only we could just club the unattainable over the head and drag him in to our cave, we'd be happy. Right?

Wrong! The Impossible to Please gets off on rejecting men. It makes him feel powerful (and frequently earns him expensive gifts). If you actually get his attention and get him to speak to you and then get him to date you, he will torture you. It may be by playing hard to get, or by calling to your attention your shortcomings (God forbid your dick is less than average); it is impossible to keep him happy for long.

Who dates this stuck up princess?

Anyone who pursues someone they can't have doesn't really want to be intimate. Do you have to kill yourself trying to please your friends? Of course not. Then why jump through flaming hoops for a lover?

Crazy as it sounds, sometimes we want to be in the dating game but are not comfortable with intimacy, so we participate in relationships that have no hope of becoming fully actualized. We look and feel like we are working hard to maintain the relationship but on some level we know this isn't going anywhere. We stay involved with The Impossible to Please as long as the suspension of disbelief stays in place and we allow ourselves to believe he may actually be emotionally available tomorrow.

Another reason we may date The Impossible to Please is because we are having a bout of low self-esteem. This boy will feed right into that, so have at it and try not to be too sarcastic when you wake up and hand the lad his walking papers.

Basically, there is no long-term reason to date The Impossible to Please, only lessons to be learned about the self.

Why Real Men Drink Straight Tequila – Part 7

I could tell this call was going to be painful pretty much right away.

The guy on the other end of the line was calm enough. However, I'm sure all of our listeners could tell his demeanor and his words didn't quite match up.

He was telling us all about the gorgeous, fascinating, spectacular man he'd started seeing, but judging by the tone of his voice, you'd think he was giving a eulogy. The guy had it bad.

"Tell us what your first impression was," I said. "How did your first evening together go? That can be very telling."

He basically described the soft-focus-rest-of-the-room-goes-quiet-while-he-turns-and-takes-a-sip-from-his-drink-then-he-cums-in-his-pants scene typically found in high-budget porn. Somehow, he'd mustered the courage to offer to buy the stranger a drink, and when he wasn't turned down, he thought he'd won the lottery.

Fast forward to the end of the night, after they've talked and flirted and he's bought him a few expensive champagne cocktails, they share a cab. He thinks he's going to score – in reality pretty boy thanks him for a great time, kisses him on the cheek, does not invite him in, but offers a phone number (schwing!). Pretty boy offers nothing toward the cab fare and our caller is left alone in the car with a raging hard on. Cue dying Pac Man noise.

"Not a home run, but not a strike out, either," I told him.

Our man calls a few days later and asks pretty boy out to dinner. He asks where his date would like to go and the pretty thing suggests the most expensive joint in town. He shells out a decent chunk of change and they have a great night. He relays that his date seems pretty into him, and when he takes him home, he kisses him for real this time and lets him feel him up through his jeans, just a little.

This goes on for a few weeks and after the 5th date, he asks him up.

He finally gets to see him naked and they have a glorious roll in the hay. To hear him describe it, it was like fireworks, a Lady Gaga concert, a new Xbox release, and Christmas, all at the same time.

By now, I was a little embarrassed for the guy. He was so unabashed about how high this pretty thing had blown his mind, which is cool, but clearly he had no idea who or what he was dealing with.

Fast forward another month. They've gone out, but with increasing frequency he's picking up the tab. They've had more sex, and it's been amazing, but he's starting to see a bored look in pretty boy's eye. He's dropped hints about things he likes, what clothes designers, what brand of shoes (who the hell is Berluti, and why are his shoes over $500?), favorite travel destinations, expensive restaurants, etc. He was telling us all over the air how much cash he's spent to keep his guy happy, but it was never enough. Soon pretty boy was pulling further and further away, and finally, stopped returning his calls entirely. And here he was today, calling for advice.

"What do I do?" the guy begged. I winced. Poor fella.

I took a deep breath and asked him if I could be straight with him. He said sure, please.

"You really want to make this guy happy?" I asked.

"Yeah, I do," he said. "More than anything."

"Then, and I hate to break it to you, buddy…introduce him to someone who has more money and lower self-esteem. That's what he's looking for."

The Younger Man

young[6]

adjective (**younger**)

having lived or existed for only a short time : *a young girl* | [as plural n.] **(the young)** *the young are amazingly resilient.*

• not as old as the norm or as would be expected : *more people were dying young.*

• [attrib.] relating to, characteristic of, or consisting of young people : young love / immature or inexperienced : *she's very **young for her age**.*

• having the qualities popularly associated with young people, such as enthusiasm and optimism: *all those who are **young at heart**.*

First, when we say "Younger Man" we're talking no older than 23. If you are a 27 year old male or younger, you can read this, but you've got a few years to go before it'll make sense. If you're over 30, this is for you.

John Derek, director of the film 10 starring the insanely hot corn-rowed Bo Derek and insanely funny Dudley Moore, was famous for his affection for young, beautiful women with a certain *look*. Ursula Andress, one of the more fabulous Cat Woman ladies on *Batman*, Linda Evans, the shoulder padded trendy blond lead on *Dynasty*, and Bo Derek were all not only wives, but leading ladies on screen thanks largely to John Derek.

John enjoyed playing the role of the older, experienced partner in his relationships. He offered these women a life they may have never attained on their own. He supported them in every way. Not all of his relationships worked, but in the end, he married another younger woman and remained married until he passed away.

Does this relationship between a man and a woman have qualities that apply to two men? Absolutely – young by any other name would smell as sweet.

Assets:

1. His body, even if he's overweight, is awesome.
2. Emotional passion. There is nothing like the naïve love of a young man.
3. His skin is probably soft and pliable, which holds everything up really nicely.
4. He is frequently easier to manipulate than an experienced man.
5. If he is having sex with you, he clearly finds older men a turn on.
6. He is easy to surprise and sate because there is so much he's never seen.

Liabilities:

1. Lack of "technique" is common if he has little SOBER sexual experience.
2. Lack of experience causes lack of problem solving skills, so you need to be the responsible party and decision maker most of the time.
3. His taste in music will probably be dramatically different than yours.
4. Lack of intellectual and emotional equality may cause you to seek others for this kind of conversation.
5. Young men change their minds more than older men and thus feel the need to try many things both personally and professionally – someone needs to pay for that.
6. There's a good chance they have no idea what they want out of life or how to get it (This last statement is very generic, there are plenty of exceptions out there).

If you are going to date a Younger Man more than a few times, you need to understand what your role is, daddy.

Do you need to be John Derek to bag a Younger Man? Sort of. John could deliver what he promised to his young ladies, namely security and a safe space to grow up. Yes, they loved him, but they were by no means intellectual or emotional peers when they met and married. He was the older, experienced person and they were the young students of life. No one but he and his wives know if they became his peers during their marriages. What we do know, is that since his passing, his last wife, Bo, has demonstrated the intelligence and grace to continue a productive life on her own, so she must have learned quite a bit.

If you like being in charge, then the Younger Man may be for you. If you like being right most of the time, the Younger Man might be for you. If you like intellectual stimulation and the emotional challenge of a peer, then you may want to reconsider.

Who would date a Younger Man long term?

LOTS OF HAPPY GUYS! Some of the happiest relationships are the byproduct of at least a ten-year gap in age. In these relationships, young men grow intellectually and emotionally under the tutelage of their partners/husbands.

In Thailand, middle-aged men still flock by the thousands to meet young malleable boys whose only interest is playing the role of supportive lover and partner. Make no mistake, they will allow you to take responsibility for pretty much everything and go with the flow as long *as you take care of the expenses*. Most younger men will not have your experience in making money, so they tend bring much less to the table.

Again, if you are John Derek, you too can grab yourself a young hottie and play big daddy. If you are an average dude with an average income and lifestyle, you can still date younger, but he needs to have expectations congruent with what you bring to the table. Just being honest, guys.

Note: It was never considered necessary to partner with an equal until the middle of the 1900's. In the revolutionary 1960's, it became popular to date as equals (take a deep breath) and create a life with someone who brought not only ideas, but also their own financial contribution to the partnership.

If you do not need the intellectual or emotional support of a peer and are interested in being in charge for either the entire relationship, or at least the first few years, a Younger Man could work for you. If you do not mind listening to tales whose outcome is predictable only to you, this could work. Last, if you are OK watching someone you care about make mistakes and letting them learn on their own, you may have the personality to enjoy the vibrancy, vitality, and outright hotness of the Younger Man.

Why Real Men Drink Straight Tequila – Part 8

"I want to report a homicide. He's going to kill me."

What a great way to start the day. I love it when they call in live and say something crazy like that. The Couple Chat radio show had become a showcase for closet romantic comedians.

"Really?" I cooed in to the mic. "How bad is it, lover?"

"I'm so confused." moaned the man on line one.

"What's your name, and where are you from?"

His name was Allen and he was from Washington, DC. His story was simple. He met and fell in love with the most beautiful man he had ever seen. He was slender, but well-muscled. His pecs were firm and his butt was like two ripe melons. He had the face of Adonis and washboard abs.

Allen must have talked for over two minutes regaling us with details of this astonishing beauty. After we all got the point, I asked him what he had done to warrant being murdered by this man.

"Well, it's like this." he started, "When we first met, one of the things that made him shy around me is that I am 15 years older than he is. By shy, I mean sexually shy. He's only 22 and I am 37. I told him I would go slow and 'educate' him. Know what I mean? Anyhow, it's been three months now."

"And has the young lad been schooled?" I asked.

"Oh, the pupil has graduated – with honors."

"So, what's the problem, Allen? Why is he angry with you?"

"He's not angry with me. As a matter of fact, he can't get enough of me. He wants me morning, noon, and night. I'm running out of semen! I literally hid in the bathroom until he fell asleep last night. I'm pale. I swear this man is sucking my blood when I'm sleeping or something."

"Allen, I'm sure I speak for our entire listening audience when I say stop bragging and either take more vitamins, or hire a stunt double.

Actually, let's see if any of our listeners feel sorry for you. Maybe some advice? Ok guys, call in if you have any sympathy for Allen at all."

You boys sure know how to get quiet when you feel like it.

CHAPTER 6

How Men Relate

To finish this book off we are visited by my co-author from Why Real Women Drink Straight Tequila – The Tao of Intimacy. R. Mordant Mahon was asked to share his thoughts on how men relate to each other because Eric and I thought it was important.

If you are going to be a successful man, having healthy connections with other men is imperative. I was curious how such a competitive gender actually pulls this off.

Clearly I am not qualified to speak bro to bro, so Mordant will take the ball from here.

This will be our final chapter. Eric and I hope you found something you can use in this little handbook. We offer no concrete solutions, but hope you found a few new doors to open and explore on your own. I bid you farewell and wish you happy hunting.

Sarina Stone
November 2013

Talk show host, serial vlogger, and author R. Mordant Mahon uses his energetic sense of humor and creative coaching style to inspire others to level up their lives. Whether entertaining and edifying on his comedic motivational talk show, "Success Freaks," or encouraging and challenging people to dance outside their comfort zones via his galvanizing keynote speeches, Mordant always succeeds in giving your mind and spirit something to chew on while putting enough laughter in your heart to make you smile out loud.

For more on R. Mordant Mahon, visit http://successfreaks.com or contact him at mordant@successfreaks.com.

Eric on how men relate

So, guys, we've been talking a lot about what happens when we meet guys and have romantic or sexual feelings for them. As much as we might like it, that doesn't cover all the bases when it comes to how men relate. We have relationships with our family members, straight friends, coworkers, and gay friends that we just don't think of that way. Those relationships are still essential to how we operate, and we thought it was worthwhile to examine what makes them tick.

My esteemed Tao-brother Mordant wrote some great stuff about man-on-man bonding (I said bonding, not bondage) for the hetero edition of this book. His insights were so spot-on that I felt remiss in not including some of his points here (plus, he's a total stud, and the party just wouldn't be complete without him). I've also included my own observations that are unique to the gay element of man-on-man interactions, so he and I can tag-team this big, hairy mound of muscles and feelings.

Okay, that sounded way dirtier than I thought it would.

Enjoy.

I Need Men.... Is That Gay?!

Here you are, at the end of a book about chivalry, wondering how you got here and why you aren't watching sports.

So far, you've read about Taoism and how to use some of the principles when dealing with sex and relationships. Now it's time to take a look at the ways guys relate to one another in day to day scenarios.

Men relate to one another in very simplistic ways.

You seem cool. Do you think I'm cool? Do you like what I like? I like what you like. Wait... are you after what I'm after? Maybe you're not so cool after all.

Simple, right? But what underlying factors drive men to become fast friends... or bitter enemies? How do our primal needs for victory and brotherhood affect our interactions with other men, here and now? And who or what teaches us that these drives are OK, that they're a crucial part of our manhood?

Eric:

While Mordant is talking about how straight guys bond, what he's saying applies to us too. We all exchange energy with the guys around us, and it's not always because we want to get naked with them. So, when that sexual element is absent, we still have to navigate all the head-butting and chest-puffing that comes to men naturally. Sure, sometimes we bat our eyelashes instead of flexing our pecs, but the end result is the same - we want to establish a pecking order and figure out who the Alphas are.

As we mature, we're told to tone it down. Ever feel that rings a little false? Sure, you want to connect with your feminine/masculine energy; it's good to remind yourself that sometimes you can ease up a little on both the macho and the flaming postures. The bonds we're talking about here - who we are as men with other men - come from our masculine energy. It's the truth we know but aren't allowed to talk about. The truth of our primal, animal natures and how those natures still serve us in the modern world.

Eric:

It's true, we sometimes still act like cavemen, even in our designer underwear and tight, sexy jeans. When it comes to deciding whether or not we want to compete with other men, there's the extra variable of sexual attraction - as your experience can attest, a guy's hotness factor can totally change your approach to how you deal with him. Straight guys don't have to worry about that (usually).

What's different for us is that when straight guys butt heads, the main way to vent that kind of aggression is trash-talking and fighting. Gay guys have the extra element of sex, and sometimes we end up locking lips with guys that drive us crazy instead of knocking fists. It's not uncommon for us to throw sex on the table as a potential solution to a disagreement, and I think this goes all the way back to the masculine need to conquer that's still encoded in our DNA.

Men relate to one another through competition and camaraderie, and it is these twin drives that forge the strongest friendships. In cliques, teams, clubs, and just hanging out, men develop a sense of who they are and what they might accomplish through their competition and camaraderie with other men. Through coaching, they receive specific examples and instruction on how to express those drives.

Camaraderie

Back in the Stone Age, lone hunter-gatherers discovered that bigger game meant bigger rewards. For primitive man, the ability to bring down a mammoth as a tribe - together - was vital to the survival of a new breed. Now, we're taught in school to keep our eyes on our own papers, but life in the Information Age is still a team sport. Writing a report for the office and you're not sure about the subject matter? Google is your friend. Got a million things to do and not enough time? Call a couple of buddies, a personal assistant, or even someone from another company associated with the project. Your band of helpful brothers ranges from the guy at the next desk to a stranger in Mumbai writing on Wikipedia.

Competition

In tribes, not only was the hunting better, so was the ability to gang up on the neighbors and take more resources - from choice fruit to the pick of the women folk, man's primal urge to possess led to tribal, civil, and national wars. Today, whether it's sucking up to the boss, out-drinking the rest of the gang, or having the cherry car on the block, competition drives us to excel against others and also against our personal history. After all, how many of us would really be motivated to get to the gym if it wasn't for that disturbingly over-six-packed guy on the cover of Men's Health or the memory of our own peak form way back in our Glory Days?

Coaching

Socrates taught Plato, Plato taught Aristotle, and Aristotle taught Alexander the Great. The chain of philosophers led to one of the greatest warriors of all time, and Alexander the Great profited from the coaching of history's greatest thinkers in his quest for world domination. Chances are, you've gotten, and are still getting, coaching from the role models in your life, and you don't have to wear a bed sheet or understand Greek to benefit.

Eric:

These facets definitely color our relationships with the men in our lives, but the way they're expressed among gay guys tends to look just a bit differently. Camaraderie is something we have going for us in spades, and we usually have an easier time talking about our feelings than our straight brothers do. When we compete, it's intense – we combine the most macho elements of sports-bonding and the most vicious Mean Girls tactics to get a leg up on one another. Coaching can look like all sorts of things, from instruction in manual labor, to mentorship in a community, to the occasional style or makeup tip. Things might look more traditional when we bond outside the tribe, but it's been my experience that straight guys come to me for the kind of advice and support his bros can't provide. I've always viewed this as a wonderful opportunity to strengthen the bonds that all men share, because we can all learn from one another.

So how does this friendship thing work for guys anyway? How can we slap a friend on the back one minute, then hip-check him out of the running the next? Days later, we're laughing about it over a couple beers with the very same buddy we threw under the bus, reminding him how we were just returning the favor. Are we truly that cavalier when it comes to our guy friends and our respect for them? Or is something more primal going on? And where do we learn this behavior—who teaches it to us?

"The success of the Rat Pack was due to the camaraderie, the three guys who work together and kid each other and love each other."
~Sammy Davis, Jr

Let's begin with Camaraderie - that sense of brotherly love and kinship from shared experiences. Football, baseball, and basketball teams, squadrons at war, dudes in a rock band, and yes, even the strippers they date, all share camaraderie. The Romans felt it as they conquered the Old World, and you felt it in Little League every time your team won or lost, whether you were pitching, fielding pop flies in the outfield, or stuck in the dugout. Camaraderie lets us belong to a whole greater than the sum of what we each bring to the table. We are part of a team, a unit, a force to be reckoned with. We can go further, climb higher, reach farther, all because we are a part of something more. And it doesn't matter whether that something is a legion of 6000 or a duo of you and your best bud. Both are stronger than solamente uno. Remember, it's always better running with a wing man - even Han Solo had Chewbacca.

It's not just in the history books, on the silver screen, or any given Sunday - Camaraderie affects you. You and every one of your buddy-buddy relationships. Take a good look at those crazy mooks you stir up trouble with. Not in your twenties anymore, and no time to hang with such rabble? How about those work buddies you're blowing off steam with at your favorite happy hour? Camaraderie.

So, what does all this brotherly love crap mean? Is it even necessary?

Funny you should ask.

Women bond through shared adversity. That's why they get so pissed off when you try to fix the latest problem they're going on about. Often, women just want you to hear them out and empathize (weird word, I know - look it up).

Men are different. We're fixers: problem... solution... beer. Easy-peasy. We get the goal line in our sights and head straight for it, often with tunnel-vision keeping us on target until we bring down our prey... or something else broadsides us. Something we never see coming. Something we're not really sure how to deal with.

It's bad enough when the truck breaks down or you drop your cell in the toilet. Even worse when it's some flunky at work...or your nemesis. Deadlines, rivals, and taxes blow. We expect the winds of misfortune to toss us about. However, it can be nearly unbearable when a sudden derailment comes, not from some foreseeable adversary that sets our Spidey-Sense a-tingling, but from within.

What happens when you let yourself down?

Again.

And you never even saw it coming.

But your friends? They all knew. They've been buzzing about it for a while. Did you listen? Naw. Hell naw! You ignored your team. Your crew. The very people you personally picked out to give you a heads up when things were about to get screwy.

Camaraderie isn't just a warm, fuzzy brotherhood that gets you to the end zone. It serves another purpose: noticing when you're about to make a bonehead play. Goading and teasing you out of behavior that works against you. Much like the government's checks and balances, your friends - well, my friends, but we'll assume your friends, too - will throw down the red flag of "WTF?" whenever you're about to pull, step in, and/or trip over something against the best interests of the United States of YOU. Annoying? Often. But trust me when I say, you want this.

You want this because it keeps you from being stupid. In the collective of your best buds' experience, someone has done the same dumbass thing you're about to do. Drunk texting the ex, streaking across the quad, picking a fight with that guy in the corner of the bar with no neck and a pool cue in one hand? Been there, done that. And while it's often expressed mockingly - "Yeah right, dude, like you can get him back/run that fast/take that guy" - it's a red flag you should take seriously.

Does this mean you have to listen to your friends' counsel every time you go wading into unsure waters? Nope. Just make an effort to be aware whenever they begin butting into your public (and even private) business. Ask yourself, is this interference - or camaraderie?

I'm not saying throw the emergency brake every time a pal blurts out, "Whoa...duuude!" Just take a moment of introspection. Look up to the sky, place your index finger against your chin, and think, Hmmmmm... is that misfortune I smell brewing? Or whatever. It doesn't really matter what you think, as long as it gives you pause enough to reconsider your course of action. If you're right and they're wrong - sometimes the case - you've lost nothing in your hesitation. But if they were right about this one... then you've given yourself time to change directions. And with enough practice, you can train yourself to notice that warning bell going off, even without your friends at your side. As you develop your maturity and your manhood, you'll start sidestepping more rough situations, and Camaraderie is a big reason why.

Iron sharpens iron, and one man sharpens (the face of) another.
~Proverbs 27:17 (ESV)

Eric:

Funny how all that Yang energy helps us stop and invoke Yin every now and then, isn't it? As fun as it is to be a daring badass all the time, looking both ways before running naked across the street really is a good idea... and a quality set of friends will stop you before you do something monumentally dumb. Hopefully.

Competition is Camaraderie's rough-and-tumble twin brother. Friendly or otherwise, you're still pitting your strength and ability against another's. And, there is a fine line between Camaraderie and Competition - sometimes more of a battle line. While the saying goes, "violence doesn't solve anything," any student of history can tell you that fighting has, in fact, solved many things. Circumstances shift, and friendships go sour. Officers who fought as comrades-in-arms during the Mexican-American War opposed each other thirteen years later, in the American Civil War. How about those friendly poker games? Lose your ass while not being allowed to save face and you might launch across the table at Terry-the-Taunter with a pair of knockout clubs in your fists.

Our need for Competition originates with civilization itself. Football arenas and baseball stadiums are based on the Roman Coliseum and its gladiatorial "games." The Celts and the Norse highly esteemed their warrior classes. For Vikings, even the afterlife was better for the bravest fighters - they got seats in Valhalla, the great feast hall. But before you begrudge Peyton Manning his star treatment at the best Hollywood tables, remember that part of the warriors' reward was to keep fighting. Even in heaven. The better the warrior, the stronger and safer the whole clan, and posthumous rewards spurred earthly competition.

Games played for fun and sport by soldiers, mercenaries, and tribesmen also trained young men. They built stamina and agility, pushing youths to become stronger, think strategically, and work as a unit. Even today's Olympic Games, meant to embody peace, prosperity, and sportsmanship, include ancient events demonstrating the abilities of a warrior (hammer toss, anyone?). The Olympic motto, "citius, altius, fortius" ("faster, higher, stronger") inspires man's competitive spirit ... and his warlike nature. I'm not advocating aggression for aggression's sake, but neither do I want you to forsake your competitive spirit. It's a huge part of who we are as men, and it helps hone our male interpersonal relationships both on and off the playing field.

For the most part, young men training for football, basketball, baseball, and hockey aren't preparing for acts of war - though dads rooting on the sidelines may tell you differently. Competition today is not a life-or-death situation (except TV wrestling - that's real, and we all know it). Nonetheless, Competition still plays a big part in how men relate to one another. We seldom have swords in hand, but we're still going for the metaphorical jugular. In sports, in business, and at play, we all want to see how others measure up to what we bring to the table... and find out where we stand ourselves.

Yeah, but what matters is "how we play the game!"

Really? What about the Race for the U.S. Presidency? In this case, it's not how you play the game that matters ... but who ends up with the prize. Doubt me? I've got over 200 years of mudslinging - all the way back to Jefferson vs. Adams - to back me up! What have you got?! Zip! Zilch! Nada! Bupkis! (Sorry. Just feeling a little competitive.)

With so much posturing, saber rattling, and trash talking, what good comes from the competitive spirit?

It's the flip side of how we learn to be men. While Camaraderie makes us part of the brotherhood, guarding us from our own folly and spurring us to group achievement, Competition teaches us to excel as individuals and take pride in what we do. The former concerns our inner nature - learning to get along with other men. The latter is the hard-knock assessment of our personal abilities, discovering our true limitations by succeeding or failing against a specific standard. Either you got it in the basket or you didn't. Your company got the bid, or those yahoos down the street did. You know you're good enough to make the cut ... or you've found out what you need to work on to get there next time.

Eric:

Among gay guys, competition can get a little screwy, since we are equally adept at building one another up as we are at tearing one another down, Showgirls style. On one hand, we have hot rugby with our bearish buddies, but on the other, we have the gym-pumped glitterati all competing to be the Fairest One of All. It's important for us to remember when we compete that we have the opportunity to challenge each other to be better versions of ourselves, and not get so caught up in the Heathers-esque nastiness of it all. Competition should be healthy and centered, not vindictive, catty, or fuel for drama.

"Coaches who can outline plays on a black board are a dime a dozen. The ones who win get inside their player and motivate." ~Vince Lombardi

Lastly, let's take a closer look at Coaching - the training process that goes into building gridiron soldiers from the milksop mamma's boys we all started out as.

Some friends of mine own a bakery business, specializing in outdoor summer festivals. They've become a go-to job for students, and they keep a waiting list for prospective employees. It's hard work - hot sun, hot ovens, grinding away long Saturdays while friends are lounging at the beach. Even so, many of their student-workers relish the experience, taking what they learn with them as they begin the rest of their lives, some sending thank-you letters to their former bosses. Others don't quite fit in with the program and are let go or quit.

Phil is a very tall man. At 6'6", he grew up playing basketball – well enough that his ability and training garnered him a scholarship and, with that, the right to play college ball as well as access to a college education. You could say the man knows the game. Due to his close proximity to several winning coaches over the years, he has become quite familiar with various training methodologies and has even developed a few strategies of his own. He now brings his coaching skills to the workplace. The result is the well-oiled machine that runs his and his wife, Rhonni's, various businesses. As Rhonni puts it, Phil will sidle up to one of their employees and, in the gruff tone of the troll beneath the billy goat's bridge, lay down the law on what they're doing wrong and how things should be done. He leaves no room for discussion.

Too harsh? Not PC enough? Some people would say so, and those same people are usually not long for Phil & Rhonni's summer-job world. But others flourish, basking in the hard-won respect and nod of approval that comes from Phil at the end of a long day of finally doing things the right way – his way.

Why is it so different for these kids, thriving in the very same work environment that causes others to wilt? They respond well to Coaching. They're willing to take direction and make adjustments on the fly, without taking the critique personally or as an attack.

In its most obvious form, people who have had personal experience with the wide, wide world of sports know what it means to be Coached. They understand that the often not-so-friendly instructions aren't an attack - they're designed to teach the player to make necessary adjustments on the road to being all they can be, while still performing the task at hand. To mold them from mama's little angel with some talent on the courts into the star athlete dad always wanted them to be. Ask any U.S. Army Drill Sergeant how this method works, and they'll likely tell you that it may not be pretty, but it gets the job done.

And for you non-athletes? An actor I know once complained to his director, "You don't tell me when I do something right! How do I know when I'm doing a good job?" The director's response: "Think of yourself as an Olympic runner and me as your coach. It's not my job to say, 'Oh, honey, you ran real fast!' It's my job to make you run faster."

Your coach is not there to "like" you - before, during, or after the game. Not even on Facebook. He doesn't care about your feelings. He wants results. And just like every muscle in your body, he will first need to tear down you, your beliefs about how a team works, and your preconceived notions about how easy it is to become a star player in order to rebuild and shape you into something you never realized you could become. A young man that he is proud to call a member of his winning team.

Those who have not had their egos dissected under the microscope of a coach – and learned to grow and ultimately win through the process – might take these caustic tirades as personal attacks. Or assume that their coach doesn't appreciate or even like them. This is just plain wrong. Can you take one more detour out of "manly" things into the world of dance? Just go with me here.

Ballet students – mostly women, but have you seen the abs on Baryshnikov lately? The man is in his 60s! - know that when their coach, their teacher, their choreographer is "mean," when they get yelled at, or repeat a step twenty times until the teacher thinks it's right, it's because they're good. And therefore, worth the teacher's time. A dancer knows it's time to quit - and who the worst student in the class is - because the teacher ignores them. Or is nice. Because it's not worth coaching a no-hoper.

The incorrect assumption, that your coach is yelling or criticizing because he doesn't like you, serves a purpose. It weeds out those who are unable or, more often, unwilling to take the very same instruction offered to their teammates and use it to get better. This holds true for your sports coach, your dad (remember all those dumbass rules that started to make sense when you turned 25?), and even your boss. Chances are, if you're getting critical feedback at work - and the opportunity to re-work projects that weren't up to snuff the first time around, or take another stab at the same type of project - someone wants you to get better. And the more you can let your ego ride and focus on taking in the instructions, the better you'll be as a part of the team, the project, or the couple.

"A gentleman is one who never hurts anyone's feelings unintentionally."
~Oscar Wilde

Eric:

Coaching is something that the gay community does pretty well, in my opinion. Granted, it's by no means perfect, but we're big on providing the next generation with tools to grow and succeed. I've known many successful gay men who made it a point to mentor younger guys in their careers, helping them learn to network and make the most of their skills. We're also huge on providing community resources to people who need them – we've all known what it feels like to wish for guidance, and while times are changing, it's a sad truth that many young gay people are still rejected by their parents, so surrogates have to step in. It's encouraging to see how willing many of us are to offer the coaching that's needed to produce quality community members.

Coaching, Competition, and Camaraderie. The trifecta of our male relationships. How can you tell when these factors are at work in your friendships, and how can you use them to find your own way of being a man?

As you have probably noticed - you are pretty sharp, after all - Coaching blurs the line between Camaraderie and Competition. It falls into both categories, and as each situation arises, our roles may have a tendency to shift. One day you're coaching a buddy on his relationship, the next you're both competing at work, or sharing camaraderie over a brew. So, part of the secret is to surround yourself with men you trust enough to give advice to and take feedback from. American entrepreneur, author, and motivational speaker Jim Rohn says, "You are the average of the five people you spend the most time with." Make sure you surround yourself with Awesome.

Like it or not, these chosen chums, consciously or subconsciously handpicked by you, are helping to mold you into whatever type of man you are becoming - whether you're ready for the lessons or not. And, trust me when I say that your mates, being the fine, upstanding gentlemen that they be, are always ready, willing, able, and happy even, to give "gentle tutoring" whenever the need arises.

Throw a woman into the mix and she might not understand what's transpiring. I'm not being chauvinistic here - I've actually seen this happen. Sarina herself thought her then-boyfriend and I were rude to one another when we first met. He's this big weightlifter and, I'm... well, a writer (To be fair, he's also a screenwriter, but I'm making a point here). There was a bit of posturing, some poking, some trash talking – you know, guy stuff. As soon as I left, she questioned him about it, almost apologizing for my behavior. He let her know there was nothing to apologize for - we were just being dudes. No problemo. The Dudes were cool. The Dudes abide.

What women might view as crude, rude, and even mean behavior, I call Giants at Play. The "giants" involved in the "friendly" tussle are usually fine. It's those tiny towns and houses caught in the fallout that always wind up suffering.

Case in point: I'm also a comedian, a member of the three-man Tortuga Twins. Our particular brand of comedy is not exactly genteel, and the same can be said for our backstage banter. We're pretty acerbic (thank you, Word-of-the-Day toilet paper), and that's fine. It's not done for the sake of those watching from the sidelines. It's part of our personal dynamic. It might even look like fun. But, don't think you can jump in, throwing your own barbs willy-nilly at any one of us, for we would then turn our mordant (also means "biting reply") attention on you, our competition turning into camaraderie against a common enemy (see what I did there?).

And our comedy one-upmanship is the adult version of something we all learned at a very young age. Something that, though often given a bad rap, plays a very important role in our upbringing. Gentlemen, I give you... Roughhousing.

"Men kick friendship around like a football, but it doesn't seem to crack. Women treat it like glass and it goes to pieces."

~Anne Morrow Lindbergh

Don't calm down. Don't stop poking your brother. And you are not in Time Out. Roughhousing is fun. From eight-year-olds giving Indian burns, to fraternity pranks, to hacking our buddy's Facebook profile, it's the childish horseplay we still do with our best mates. Is it really beneficial to adults? I mean really? Again, I have to come back at you with an emphatic yes!

When we're young, Roughhousing allows us to stretch our muscles and push our boundaries in a relatively safe environment. The first time we broke a lamp inside… or wrecked our sister's bike outside, we learned how far we could take things. This taught us to temper our horseplay, without consequences more dire than a few trips to the ER – and hey, ambulances have awesome sirens! Better to learn how much is too much while we're still on our parents' insurance.

As boys, most of our coaching came from our dads; or father figures in single-parent households. He was the one who made sure things never went too far. When they did, the appropriate amount of punishment was doled out. Dad also played damage control, picking up the broken pieces of ma's favorite figurine and teaching us about the wonders of Superglue and a homemade "I'm sorry" card. He even took in stride the beatings we gave him after coming home from that cool martial arts movie.

Think about puppies, biting and gnawing at your fingers. Sure, they're teething. But get them playfully riled up and sometimes the chomping comes a little hard and hungry. A quick yelp from the master (you, not them) and a gentle pop on the snoot (theirs, not yours), and they learn. Not anthropomorphizing (you got that one) here, but they often appear apologetic. As with animals, so with men. It's sharp reminders from our dads and coaches that teach us how hard we can bite before it's not ok.

That's camaraderie's side of roughhousing. On the competition front, it's different. Here, you learn to push past your limitations by playing with bigger dogs. Tennis player Jimmy Conners' number one piece of advice to newcomers on the court? "Play with better players. You'll learn more." We start by losing - a lot (unless we're the oldest brother and the biggest kid on the block). Coming out on the short end of the roughhousing stick teaches us to look for our own ways to victory: whether it's being faster, smarter, stronger, or the kid who best invokes the adults' sympathy when the fight gets broken up.

All this was pre-schooling for the more formal coaching we got, once old enough to learn under an adult other than our parents. At home, we learned to enjoy both camaraderie and competition from a very early age. This not only whetted our appetites for greater games to come, it also put us in training for how men relate to one another.

To pray for courage that we might encourage others.

To pray for the forgiveness of others,

That we may be forgiven ourselves…

This is the Heart of ancient Knighthood.

~Sir R. I. Tulak

So we've discussed Camaraderie, Competition, Coaching, and Roughhousing. We've seen how these things are ingrained in the male psyche and put into use in our day to day lives. How does this relate to the Tao of Chivalry, and why should we actively use these drives when interacting with other men?

You already know about jousting, knights belonging to tables of various shapes and sizes, noble quests for eternal glory, fair maidens, lordly titles and high-end real estate. They were engaging in what we now call fair play, good sportsmanship, being a gentleman. Back in the 11th century, chevaliers ("knights") thought this stuff was so important they wrote it down, and that's where "chivalry" got its name. (Yes, those words are related.)

The basics of knighthood are so ingrained in us that you probably could write the Code of Chivalry yourself, given a few minutes to think about it.

1. Take care of weak people; defend your family, your friends and your nation

2. Be as strong as you can and use your strength for good

3. Fight for justice and your beliefs

4. Be loyal to the people and ideals you live by

5. Have faith and be willing to defend it

6. Be humble, "tell the deeds of others before your own"

7. Be generous

8. Be a good example

9. Be courageous, and willing to make sacrifices while carrying out this code

10. Do all this, not for personal gain, but because it's the right thing to do.

All these go hand in hand with the idea of "Noblesse Oblige" – the idea that the more you have and the stronger you are, the greater your responsibility to give back. Bill Gates, at one time the richest man in the world, is really into spending billions on basic preventative health care in developing nations. WWE Superstar John Cena? Also totally down with kids with terminal diseases, helps out through the Make-A-Wish Foundation. And you - what do you care about that you can spend some time, some money, and some of your personal power lending a hand?

Think about the kind of guy you want to be. How you want your co-workers, your guy friends, your teammates, your spouse, and your children to talk about you. As always - regardless of your upbringing, what you've learned from coaches and mentors, and even your DNA - the choice of who you are is ultimately up to you, my friend. Now that you know more about why you act the way you do, you can make the choice to be someone dudes want to hang with and others admire. Or you can play a schmuck who takes advantage of the weak, pushes around the beta-dogs, and tags & bags those who happen to be a little too drunk to be making good choices. Harsh? You know someone who's done it. And it's up to you whether that's you - ever, or ever again.

It all comes back to how you treat others, and whether or not you're secure enough in your own manhood to lay a little Noblesse Oblige down for a fellow human being. Will you not only lend a hand to the obviously less-fortunate, or to someone whose pants you want into, but also allow someone whose life is lacking spotlight-time their moment of glory? Think about volunteering for the Special Olympics or a cause you care about, but also consider pulling back your shine a little if your shy buddy is garnering a little attention from a mutual object of attraction. Know when to compete, know when to coach, and know when to be a brother.

Noble pursuits all. It basically comes down to what kind of man you want to be. And, how you want to relate to other men as you play out this ultimate Super Bowl Game we call Life.

Eric's Conclusion

I have to say, Mordant's words ring pretty true to me, and while sometimes the temptation exists to believe gay guys operate by a totally different set of rules, I think he's touched on some universal man-truths here. It might not look the same on the surface, but these are all fundamental underpinnings that govern a lot of our behavior when we interact with other men, whether or not we're trying to sleep with them. We're a little more touchy-feely (okay, a lot more touchy-feely), but ultimately we're doing the same stuff. Being aware of where those drives come from gives us the opportunity to act with greater intention and build stronger bonds with all of the men in our lives.

Our need for chivalry runs as deeply as our need for romantic intimacy. Without understanding where we fit within the fabric of manhood, how can we hope to understand what we offer to our partners? Ages ago, we learned to be men through specific rites of passage, but times have changed, and it seems that boys are becoming men later and later in life, or sometimes, never becoming men at all.

We all need each other to be the best we can be, so we can learn and grow together. I've come to accept that I have a responsibility to enrich the lives of those with whom I surround myself by being the best possible example of happiness and fulfillment I can be. I know of course I don't have it all figured out, which is why I look for others to enrich my experience with their own teachings. Partnerships are then created, in which we help one another realize our shortcomings and how to grow beyond them.

Heed the call to chivalry, my brothers. In learning to be the best possible man you can be, you will attract the very best in friends and lovers, who in turn will pass along what you have taught – and if you're lucky, they'll teach you a thing or two in return. If we can all inspire and nurture one another for long enough, maybe people will stop saying that chivalry is dead, that nice guys finish last, and that men only want one thing. Maybe more of us will simply express gratitude for all of the wonderful men we have in our lives.

Eric Thurnbeck

January 2014

www.ingramcontent.com/pod-product-compliance
Lightning Source LLC
Chambersburg PA
CBHW030019290326
41934CB00005B/403